ARE YOU STILL BELOW?

ARE YOU STILL BELOW?

The Ford Marina Plant, Cork
1917 - 1984

MIRIAM NYHAN

The Collins Press

Published in 2007 by
The Collins Press
West Link Park
Doughcloyne
Wilton
Cork

British Library Cataloguing in Publication Data

Nyhan, Miriam A.
   Are you still below? : a history of the Ford Marina Plant,
Cork, 1917-84
   1. Ford Motor Company. Marina Plant - History 2. Automobile
industry and trade - Ireland - Cork - History
   I. Title
   338.4'7629222'0941956

ISBN-13: 9781905172498

Contents

For my parents, and for Sonny Scully —
who, I believe, always drove a Ford

Picture Credits:

Acknowledgements

Without those who agreed to take part in the collection of oral histories, this study would have been impossible. I am eternally grateful to those who shared their recollections of Henry Ford & Son Limited and I feel privileged to have been a participant in documenting their memories. Many thanks to Maurice Ahern; Oliver Barriscale; Bobby Broderick; Dominic Carey; Eddie Cleary; Michael Corkery; Donal Creamer; Derry Creedon; John Curran; Frank Dillon; Vaunie Downey; Bob Elliot; Denis Forde; Ken Galvin; Pat Gillen; Max Hayes; Paddy Hayes; Tim Healy; Billy Hurley; Eddie Kehelly; Noreen Kelly; Denis Manning; Gus McLaughlin; Denis McSweeney; Tom Morrissey; Michael Mulconry; Eddie Mullins; Frank Norberg; Arthur O'Callaghan; John O'Callaghan; Bill O'Donnell; Michael J. O'Donoghue; Tom A. O'Donoghue; Jim V. O'Donovan; and Michael Quinlan. It is with sadness that I note that at least five of the people I met in the course of research for this project have since died. Arthur Owens, Con Murphy, Jack Broderick and Jack Fives passed away after I recorded their reminiscences with them. Also, I had the opportunity to meet the late historian Ford R. Bryan in Michigan in 2003. It was an honour and indeed a pleasure to meet someone who was such an authority on Henry Ford and the Ford family history.

Similarly, I would like to acknowledge the assistance of the Judith E. Endleman, Laura Mancini and Linda Skolarus (Benson Ford Research Center, Dearborn, Michigan); Michelle Graham (Ford Motor Company Archives, Dearborn, Michigan); Bob Montgomery (Royal Irish Automobile Club Archive, Dublin); Brian McGee (Cork Archives Institute, Cork); the staff of Cork City Library; the staff of Cork County Library; SIPTU, Cork (Branch 6); Piaras Mac Éinrí (Irish Centre for Migration Studies, University College Cork); RTÉ Archival Staff; Bríd Crowley (Audio Visual Services, University College Cork); Rev. Steward Foster (England) the staff of the National Archives (Dublin); T.P. Brady (Arklow); Gearóid Ó Crualaoich; the staff of Boole Library, University College Cork and most particularly the librarians in 'Special Collections'; Dermot Keogh; J.J. Lee; Enda Delaney; Charlotte Holland; Maurice Cronin; Eddie Murphy; Terry O'Regan; Anne O'Leary; Paddy Byrne; Eddie Nolan; Ian Heaslip; Ann and Gene Walker; Michael McCarthy; Derrick Wilkins; John Brennan (New York); Pat Butler; Tom Sheridan of Sheridans Garage Waterford; Andy Bielenberg; Donal O'Driscoll; all at The Collins Press; and the staff of Henry Ford & Son Limited, both past and present.

Finally, I would like to thank my many friends; and Clare, Emma and Eileen, and most especially my parents for their unfailing support.

Nomenclature

Throughout the text the terms the Marina, Henry Ford & Son Limited and Fords are used to refer specifically to the Cork Ford operation unless otherwise stated. Any references to other Ford entities (e.g. Ford of Europe, Ford Motor Company {England}) are made explicitly. Similarly, references to Henry Ford and Henry Ford II as individuals are made in an exact manner so as to prevent confusion. Because of the frequency of their occurrences, the terms listed above (and that of the 'Dagenham Yanks') forgo any stylistic differentiation in the text.

Abbreviations

BFRC: Benson Ford Research Center at The Henry Ford, Dearborn, Michigan

NAI DT: National Archives, Dublin, Department of Taoiseach files

NAI DTI: National Archives, Dublin, Department of Trade and Industry files

HFL: The archival holding of records at Henry Ford & Son Limited, Cork. The format of references is that the accession number is provided firstly, followed by the document title (presented in single quotation marks) and the date of the document.

SIPTU Cork, Branch 6 files: This refers to the records held at SIPTU's (Services Industrial Professional & Technical Union) office at Lapps Quay, Cork. This union was founded in part by the ITGWU (Irish Transport and General Workers Union). The format of the references made from this holding is as follows: the file name is provided immediately following 'SIPTU Cork, Branch 6 files', where possible, the document name (presented in single quotation marks) is then presented, followed by the date of the document.

[Name] interviewed [date] or [Name] interview: Refers to one of the 35 interviews undertaken as part of the research. The text of the interview extracts is only altered to clarify meaning. This collection of oral interviews will, in the future, be donated to a suitable archive. Any clarifications of meaning of words/phrases are only made in the first occurrence. The date of interview is only provided in the first reference to the interview. See Appendix (iv).

Irish Centre for Migration Studies – 'Breaking the Silence': Refers to the oral archive of the 'Breaking the Silence' project carried out by the Irish Centre for Migration Studies based in University College Cork (http://migration.ucc.ie). The name of the interviewee referenced is provided in the relevant endnote.

Foreword

Ford has been a presence in my life for as long as I can remember. My earliest motoring memories from the 1950s are of going to the beach at Fountainstown, or Youghal, in a Model Y or 'Baby Ford'. I recall, too, some epic excursions to drag hunts in Kenmare or Liscarroll – men, boys, dogs and all, piled into a Ford V8 saloon that my Dad had borrowed for the day. Dad loved the independence and sense of adventure that a car gave him. He daydreamed, I suspect, of the day when he would get the next best model. 'If I won the Sweep …', was a common phrase he would use to begin sharing with us his latest 'dream'. He took my brother and me to see the latest new model launches at dealerships in Cork, or to see the extraordinary displays of cars and machinery at the Cork Summer Show. Ford was the only significant show in town, in those days. I remember the Consul 315 and the chic Consul Capri. I remember the Anglia being launched in Primrose Yellow at Transit Motors' showroom on MacCurtain Street.

From our lofty perch above the city, we had a view down river to the Marina, where we could see the white walls and black roof of the industrial giant stretched along the banks of the Lee. We could also see the City of Cork Steam Packet Company's *Innisfallen* when she berthed at Penrose Quay. To my young mind, there appeared a connection between the two. My Dad's brothers, Paddy and Jim, had worked at the Marina, but, like many another, had felt the lure, or the push, to go on the steamer to 'Dag-num,[1] to work at the new Ford giant plant along the Thames in Essex. The vocabulary of Cork people at that time was sprinkled with names and places with which they felt completely comfortable, names and places such as Ford, Marina, Dagenham, Fishguard, Thames, Barking, Paddington, *Innisfallen*. Cork and Dagenham became symbiotic, almost like Buda and Pest, though something wider than the Danube separated them. For thousands, taking the *Innisfallen* to Fishguard, and the train from there to Paddington, to get a 'start' in the next few days at 'Dag-num', was as normal as taking the bus to Ballyphehane to work on the newest housing estate.

Ford men lived around us at home. They always seemed to have that little extra in monetary terms. A job on the Marina with Ford, or at the neighbouring Dunlop plant, meant financial security in relative terms, at a time when employment in the city was, for the most part, casual.

My mother was devout, and she wore a path to St Augustine's church, to the Mother of Good Counsel altar, to pray for all her flock, whatever the challenge – exam, sickness, wedding or job prospect. I'm sure she prayed there the day I went for my Ford interview in 1971. She could scarcely conceal her joy when I was given a job, as to her mind, I was made for life. In many ways, she was right; not least, because I have worked for the company ever since. Ford shaped me, educated me, directed me and moulded me as a business man. I share those influences with some of the most successful business people in Cork, some who stayed longer term with Ford, others who ventured far and wide afterwards. All acknowledge the momentous influence Ford had on their careers and businesses.

My overriding impression of the Marina on that first day, 4 October 1971, was of bustle, activity, huge numbers of men and material on the move with a purpose, the noise, but above all, the inexorable grind of the production line. There was only one rule; don't stop the line. It was a like a small town, eight acres under roof; behind the guarded gates, it appeared self-sufficient. It had its own 300 metres of wharf, its own cranes to load or unload ships, its own workshops for fitters, electricians or millwrights. In the 'Cut and Sew', 25 tailors made the seat covers and upholstery. At the time, the Marina produced Escort, Escort Van, Cortina, Transit van and D-series trucks at the rate of 80 units per day. This was considered heresy in production efficiency terms by those who were quickly converting plants to produce just one model. It is amusing to hear experts now extolling the virtues of flexible production lines as the way forward in optimising the match between supply and demand. The 'beat-ahs'[2] were doing it forty years ago.

I started as a security man, doing the hum-drum work that that implies. I worked shifts for eight months. The plant was racing to meet demand, working an extra hour per shift; I worked that too. They worked Saturday mornings; I did that as well. Shift-rate, time-and-a-half, double-time – I couldn't, or so it appeared to me as a single man, spend the money that was coming in so fast as salary. I was gaining a wealth of experience as well, that would stand to me the rest of my career, not least how to relate to and get on with a variety of people in a multitude of situations.

I was promoted to the sales department after eight months, where I daily felt the heat of a competitive, performance-oriented business. However, the plant reflected the pulse of the company's daily life, and we were joined to it at the hip. Everybody at the Marina was involved in feeding the line or in shipping and selling its produce. The sense of a beat or cadence entered all our lives, from a consciousness of punctuality and commitment to delivery, to the pre-ordained summer holiday schedule, the discipline of order and control.

It is no surprise that a wide variety of pastimes and interests developed among people at the Marina. It helped to break the 'tyranny' of the line's rhythm, giving something to daydream, and to engage in a chat with colleagues about, during the day. I sensed that very many who worked there did so for the lure of the good money and constancy of employment, as they were intelligent and educated beyond their chosen occupation. Their outlets were myriad, from philanthropy to team sports, drama to music.

Slagging,[3] accurate nick-names, and a tireless sequence of practical jokes were features of life there. A very strong bond exists between those who have ever worked at the Marina. Even after retirement, resignation or, unfortunately, redundancy, Fordmen always enquire how things were going in the plant, how so-and-so was getting on, and in which department you were now working. The ubiquitous greeting, which I hear to this day, and which inspired the title of this book, is 'Are you still below?'

When we came to celebrate the centenary of Ford Motor Company in 2003, we realised that the number of people remaining who had memories of the Marina was reducing inexorably. The pain of the closure of the plant in 1984 had stung deeply, and had made a treatment of its history something to be deferred. I believed that we had an obligation to record that history and to conserve for posterity the memories and stories of the vibrant community who spent a significant portion of their lives at the Marina.

We contacted Miriam Nyhan, who was at that time in the process of doing a Masters thesis in UCC's Department of History on social housing in Cork city in the late nineteenth and early twentieth century. I persuaded her that I had a far better topic; and so she agreed to take on the research which has led to this book. During the course of the research, she discovered the phenomenon known as the 'Dagenham Yank.'[4] This has opened up a world of Irish migration studies and research in Britain and the US. Miriam and I spent many long hours discussing and discovering Ford topics, from the Ford family to Ballinascarty, from Fair Lane to Dearborn. I confess to having done most of the talking; Miriam was the patient, avidly leading listener, a skill she put to great use in recording interviews with many of our former colleagues, and which are preserved for posterity.

Henry Ford & Son Limited remains a leading company in Ireland and, this year, celebrates its ninetieth anniversary in Cork, the home of Henry Ford's ancestors, paternal and maternal. We like to consider Ford an Irish company, with a very large American branch. I commend this book. It is a work of scholarship, but also one which attempts to preserve the rich human component of an enterprise that dominated Cork industrial life for the better part of the twentieth century.

Denis McSweeney
Cork, April 2007

A view from Montenotte of the newly-built Ford plant in 1921, from the perspective of Tivoli and Montenotte dwellers.

Preface

'What difference does it make to suffering humanity if a man in Cork who used to wear a kerchief about his neck is now wearing a collar? Changing from a kerchief to a collar is only a symbol. But it is an important symbol.'
Henry Ford, 1926 [1]

'Our plant at Cork was the first Ford manufacturing facility to be established by my grandfather outside North America. In a sense, it marked the start of Ford as a productive multinational enterprise.'
Henry Ford II, 1977 [2]

This year it is exactly nine decades since Henry Ford chose Ireland to host his newest venture in the world of vehicle manufacture. The 1917 announcement heralded a very exciting development for the country's economy and was broadly welcomed locally. The 67 years to follow Henry Ford's Irish experiment would see in the establishment of a new state; another global conflict and countless other economic, political and social developments which would impact on his endeavour. Finally, in 1984, the magnate's endowment to the city of Cork took a massive blow with the closure of the plant. While this event had an irreversible impact on life on the Marina, the Ford-Cork link had not been totally severed. Even today, the sales and distribution of Ford cars for the Irish market takes place only a short distance from Cork's former Ford site.

The pages that follow chronicle a history: a history of the workings of the plant of Henry Ford & Son Limited as it was based on the Marina in Cork between 1917 and 1984. It traces the evolution of a type of identity which grew out of (and around) this entity. It outlines the ebbs and flows of life in this community within a community. From the very beginning of this research the pervasive effect of the closure of the plant was striking. Thus, a primary aim of this study was to document the years prior to the factory closure so that 1984 could be looked at with some degree of historical context. The format used is mainly chronological; but the narrative is interwoven with thematic aspects of the Ford operation in Cork. A wide variety of sources were consulted: from oral interviews and company archives, official statistics and surveys, to biographies, novels, newspapers, trade directories and academic publications.

The history of this plant starts out by going back to a pivotal set of circumstances which would fundamentally alter Cork's economy a half century later; and for a period of almost seven decades. To take this story from the beginning means recounting the early life of the son of an Irish migrant, who grew up on a Michigan farm in the 1860s. The boy in question was Henry Ford, who was the son of William and Mary (Litigot) Ford. William, along with other family members, had left Ballinascarthy, County Cork, in 1847. Henry's mother, Mary, was the adopted daughter of one Patrick Ahern who was born in Fair Lane (now Wolfe Tone Street) Cork, in 1804. Ahern, it seems, may have worked as a butcher in Cork before joining the British Army. Whether he used military service only as a means to get to North America is not clear, but he ended up in the vicinity of Dearborn, Michigan in 1834.

Henry Ford's father, William, who left Ballinascarthy for North America at the height of the Famine in 1847.

When people talk of Henry Ford's Irish links they usually, for logical reasons, look back to the Ford side of the family and Ballinascarthy. And, while it is clear that even Henry Ford himself took an interests that aspect of his heritage, it is possible that it was actually the maternal connection – through Patrick Ahern – which was more significant for the young Henry. When Henry's parents married they had moved into the home of Patrick Ahern and his wife. So, when Henry was born in 1863 it was in the Ahern household that he took his first breaths. It was in the house of this Fair Lane man that the intellect and outlook of the man who revolutionised transport for the masses, and methods of mass production, was moulded. One should not underestimate the influence Patrick Ahern may have had on the young Henry as he grew up; most especially when Henry's mother (Patrick Ahern's adopted daughter) died when he was just thirteen years of age.

Are we to assume that Henry's visit to Cork and to Fair Lane in 1912 was insignificant, when just five years later the first purpose-built Ford entity outside of North America was located in the city? And, how can we believe that Henry Ford's Dearborn mansion – which was called 'Fair Lane'– was not a tribute to Ahern? Around 40 years later, in 1955, the Ford company would use the name of Henry Ford's home

(i.e., Patrick Ahern's birthplace) for a new model of Ford cars and with that the 'Fairlane' was enshrined into automobile history globally. But most do not know the exact origin of this acknowledgment to Patrick Ahern, a man who Henry Ford presumably grew to love and idolise as a boy and an adolescent. The migration of Henry Ford's ancestors from Ireland represents a miniscule part of what became the renowned Irish diaspora. But, not many offer as impressive an example of the legacy of the Irish migration as that of two Corkmen: Patrick Ahern and William Ford.

An unidentified gentleman at the remains of William Ford's home in Madame, Ballinascarthy, County Cork, as it stood in 1954. Even these ruins have, by now, disappeared.

In building up the context of the decision-making process, it was important to explore the character of the city at the time when the plant was established. This survey of Cork provides an examination of the conditions that led to the establishment of the first purpose-built Ford manufacturing plant outside North America. It is significant to consider why, ultimately, Cork was selected as the guinea pig in Henry Ford's then experimental, overseas expansion programme. With this in mind, one well-known Fordman, Walter Hayes', observation with regard to the role of sentimentality and the Ford Company's strategic development is worth noting:

> Edmund Burke once observed that a great empire and little minds go ill together, but empires are often assembled in a haphazard fashion, with chauvinism as their most distinctive feature. In its earliest days Ford had a factory in Copenhagen, Denmark, for the same reason it had one in Cork, Ireland: sentiment. Henry Ford built a tractor plant in southern Ireland in 1917 because his father had come to the United States from County Cork, and Copenhagen was chosen as a location in 1919 because William Knudsen [Ford executive] had been born there; coincidently, both plants produced their first vehicle in the same day, July 3, 1919.[3]

To begin, the study will look at Henry Ford the individual, for whom the progression into the tractor business and to Ireland was very much a personal mission. This is highlighted by, among other things, his move in setting up an entirely separate tractor company called Henry Ford & Son Incorporated in 1915 where the shareholders were all members of his immediate family. But there are many considerations that have to be factored into assessing the decision to set up in Ireland – and more especially the city of Cork – in 1917. And, there is one crucial factor that needs to be given due note prior to all other influences. This is the First World War. The advance into tractor production was greatly hurried as a result of the conflict. The study will then focus on the establishment of Ford's Cork operation and examine the events of the first decade of the plant's existence. While chronological to a large extent, this explores the antagonisms that influenced life on the Marina in these early, but important, years. It demonstrates how the Ford plant established itself within the spectrum of the existing political and social world into which it had been born. The chapter's title reflects the manner by which the site was fundamentally altered from the green fields of the city's racecourse to the home of pioneering industrial processes on this side of the Atlantic in a relatively short period of time.

There exists today in Cork an ever-diminishing lore pertaining to the history of the Ford enterprise in the city. In its present form, it consists mainly of anecdotal descriptions of a group of people referred to as the 'Dagenham Yanks'. This colloquial term was widely applied to the thousands of individuals and families who migrated from Cork to employment in Ford in England over four decades, dating from the early 1930s. Historians have hitherto largely ignored the significance of this diaspora and this work examines this minute group of what became a monumental Irish exodus to Britain during the twentieth century. The institution of the 'Detroit of Europe' at Dagenham and thus the background to migration to Britain from Cork occupy a significant part of the story. The events that would lead to the need to migrate in order to maintain continuity of employment are placed in the broader social and economic context of the years in question. Along with this, the overarching way in which the story of the Dagenham Yanks fits into the history of life in the Cork plant is explored.

The study then examines what life was actually like for a worker in Ford's Cork plant. In the course of research, interviews with approximately 40 individuals who had connections with the Cork operation were undertaken; and countless casual discussions contributed. The material provided in these reminiscences are an important part of the narrative and are utilised in an attempt to humanize the history of the Ford operation in Cork.

So, essentially, the focus is people's memories. Sometimes it's also about their father's memories, or their uncle's or those of a friend. It is about their work and their working lives: arguably the single biggest influence on the lives of people in the last century. Condensing descriptions and stories, covering sometimes a period of 40 years, into a relatively brief conversation, can only present an incomplete picture. But it is a picture, at least, and it can also provide a testament for those colleagues who were not afforded an opportunity to document their story. The oral history collector Kevin Kearns observes that oral 'historians are haunted by the obituary page. Every death represents the loss of a potential narrator and thus an absolute diminution of society's collective historical memory'.[4] With this in mind, I became aware that in some cases there was a fast approaching onus to relate facts for the permanent written record with a sense of responsibility and sometimes urgency.

The reliability of the information was gained by questioning numerous people about the same topics and themes. The interviews served two purposes: firstly, they provided an oral history of the workings of Henry Ford & Son Limited and in doing so revealed insights that could only come from people who worked there; secondly, and no less importantly, the interviews acted as a social process in documenting certain (not all) memories of plant life.

Almost all those interviewed held impressively long tenures with the company – figures of 40-plus years were not at all uncommon. In a climate where a secure, reliable job (which guaranteed a pension) was the aspiration, this dedication would come as no surprise. But, it also reflects an immense level of loyalty and commitment to the firm to ensure that such a sizeable proportion of its employees were happy to remain with the company over many decades; and often over generations. The interviews quickly began to demonstrate that in working for Fords in Cork one automatically became part of a micro-community: one employee made the observation that the plant was 'just like a town'. Exploration of this feature was quickly identified as something worthwhile.

Finally, the economic considerations that led to the closure of the factory in July 1984 are explored. From the outset, the emotion stirred when the plant closure was mentioned was most intriguing. And for obvious reasons, the subject formed a sizeable part of questioning in the interviews undertaken. In each interview, *the* definitive answer as to why assembly was withdrawn from the Marina was sought. It became clear that the reasons for the closure were exclusively based on economic considerations – a decidedly boring but logical explanation for the move. Yet the sentiments and viewpoints surrounding the event were human, impassioned reactions and deserve as much attention as the fundamentals of profitability and loss. Also, it was interesting to note that when forced to recall something that exceeded the realm of close personal experiences (or was perhaps something painful to relate), many relied on the shared discourse that took place in their locality after the event happened – rather than provide direct recollections of the event itself. This was undoubtedly a trait of many of the interview recollections pertaining to the cessation of assembly on the Marina.

It has been suggested that Fords tended to dominate Cork's economy and that there was a developing tendency for the city to rotate around the company. This is probably true to some extent but it would also seem unsurprising in a city the size of Cork and with the economic nature of Ireland being as it was in these decades. The arrival of an arm of the Ford Motor Company changed many things in Cork. It marked the beginning of the shift of international capital towards the establishment of manufacturing industry in the economic periphery. But more important for those who worked there- to use the words of one well-known former Ford employee, Donnacha O Dulaing – at finishing time, 'the prosperity of Cork poured out the gates onto the crowded quays. Yes indeed, Henry Ford and his assembly lines gave back to Cork much more than his ancestors had taken from Ballinascarthy'.[5] This book examines the implications of that assertion.

Why Cork?

'My ancestors came from near Cork, and that city, with its wonderful harbour, has an abundance of fine industrial sites. We chose Ireland for a plant because we wanted to start Ireland along the road to industry. There was, it is true, some personal sentiment in it.'

Henry Ford, 1926 [1]

'I understand that you are leaving for America on Saturday and that you hope to be able to arrange with Mr Henry Ford that he shall manufacture and supply six thousand farm tractors and spares to be shipped to the Ministry here in England, so that we can put them together in time to be of service for the 1918 Food Production Programme. If Mr. Ford will help in this way I believe he will be rendering a great service to this country.'

C. Addison, Minister of Munitions, 1917 [2]

On 8 August 1912 the Cork daily newspapers carried headlines regarding the landing of the motor boat, *Detroit,* at Queenstown (now Cobh) late the evening before, having made an arduous journey across the Atlantic in 21 days, sixteen hours. *Detroit* was greeted with a hearty welcome by the crowds who had gathered on the shore and the well-wishing Kinsale fishermen, many of whom went aboard. Local vessels had escorted her along the inner waters of the harbour. Captain Day thanked the gathering for their enthusiastic reception and proclaimed of his lineage, 'It is not all American, as I have some Irish blood in my veins too, and I am proud of it'.[3] Coincidently, on that very next day, a businessman who hailed from near the Michigan state capital was making a journey to those very same shores as *Detroit* and to those of his own forefathers. This entrepreneur was met with no welcoming committee or ostentatious greeting. He quietly disembarked a sailing, with his wife and son, to the city his family had left almost 60 years previously in search of a better life. The businessman was a man called Henry Ford.

Starting with the genealogical link as a direct influence in selecting Cork is very purposeful here. The Ford family's history was undoubtedly to the forefront of Henry Ford's mind as a man who was absolutely consumed by an overbearing interest in his genealogy: this is most amply demonstrated by the extensive projects, expense and energy that he contributed – be it intermittently – to the compilation of an accurate family tree.[4] It has been noted that he 'liked the idea of a great factory rising in the land of his ancestors' and that 'he felt that his most signal contribution to the welfare of Ireland would be the implanting of a flourishing engineering industry in that country'.[5] This is not to say that it was the only reason or that he was on a sentimental crusade that would overly bias him in one way or another. Henry Ford was a businessman and a very successful one at that. Here was a man who, by

*The son of an Irish migrant, who would become one of the most influential
figures of the twentieth century. Henry Ford (1863-1947)*

1914, was responsible for the production of about half the output of the American automobile industry. But, it is not insignificant that as early as 1913 Henry Ford had his British representative looking for a suitable plant site in Cork.[6]

The city of Cork to which Henry Ford arrived in 1912 was obviously a very different city to that which his family had left the century before. The urban plights that faced all cities in the era in question were all too apparent in the case of Cork and it seems that these concerns were of special interest to Henry Ford at the time. The philosophies that had been espoused by Ebenezer Howard's Garden City Movement were certainly familiar to the automobile magnate.[7] In broader terms too, it is abundantly evident that Henry Ford claimed to hold a basic ethos aimed at improving the lot of the lower classes. Of course, the notion of a car that would be attainable by the masses was greatly espoused by the Ford company. And anyway, philanthropic schemes were increasingly in vogue: the work of Sir Edward Cecil Guinness' Iveagh Trust in London and Dublin are a well-known example of this close to home.[8] Of course this outlook made very good business sense where a large labour pool and a healthy workforce were of utmost benefit to any potential employer. Yet there is sufficient evidence to suggest that this ran a little deeper here. Henry's notion of contributing substantial employment in the land his relatives had left under less than ideal circumstances seemed to hold great appeal for him. And, the sentiments of a communication, written over a decade later, would seem to make it clear that he was aware of the linkages between employment opportunities and living standards:

> I called Mr Ford's attention to the housing shortage in Cork, but that did not draw any response from him other than 'I will provide the work and that matter will regulate itself'.[9]

By the end of the nineteenth century, Ireland was in some respects pretty developed.[10] One eminent historian points out that about half the agricultural and industrial output was exported and that Irish linen, liners, whiskey, beer and biscuits were all world famous.[11] Ireland then was a regional part of the most advanced European economy; Britain. So, many economic and legal structures were favourable for industry and trade – especially those geared towards the British market. But, it is irrefutable to state that even by 1900 the conditions needed for any significant level of industrialisation were problematic in Ireland. Factors such as the population decline, the land system, the political instability, the lack of natural resources and the costs involved in exporting, all combined to make Ireland a risky economy into which businessmen might invest. And, with this in mind, it seems that the Ford move into Ireland is even more notable and exceptional in its wider significance. David Jacobson's survey of the arrival of Fords to Cork puts this in a broader 'Ford' context when he poses the following question:

In view of the fact that the Ford enterprise in those early years spread to areas like Canada and Latin America, where high tariffs and large markets justified local assembly, and to England and the Continent, where transport cost-saving and rapidly increasing sales also justified local plants, why did Ford set up in Ireland, where sales were relatively low, the potential market limited, and the distance from potential export markets relatively great?[12]

Let us explore some of the issues raised in asking this exact question.

Early twentieth-century Cork possessed an economy that was characterised by its reliance on agriculture. In fact, agriculture essentially sustained many of the industrial ventures in the food and drinks sectors in particular. This was not a unique Cork phenomenon. Ireland as a whole was still an overwhelmingly rural market. Most of Ireland's industry was situated in the northern province of Ulster. By 1911 the situation was that in the six counties that became Northern Ireland (predominantly in the vicinity of Belfast) about 35 per cent of the labour force was involved in industry – which was not far off the British level. In the remaining counties industrial labour was only estimated at thirteen per cent of the total.[13]

While Cork city had never been a major centre for heavy industry, approximately twenty per cent of the male population was employed in the manufacture and transport sectors by 1901.[14] Yet, less than thirteen per cent of skilled men and less than half of the total male workforce were employed in large-scale establishments.[15] The skilled male workforce was, for the most part, not employed in factory settings but instead in workshops, or as contractors, in the various trades.[16] Nonetheless, the late years of the 1800s had seen the establishment of various factories involved in feather-dressing, tobacco, biscuit-bakery, footwear, clothing and match manufacture. Trade directories are a useful source in listing the business and industrial concerns of the locality.[17] By about 1919 in Cork city the wool industry employed 1,800; saw-milling and munitions, 1,500; weaving and spinning, 1,000; brewing and distilling, 600; dock work, 500; flour milling, 400; engineering, 350; shirt-making, 250; bacon curing, 250; boot and shoe manufacture, 400; jams and preserves, 180; and coach building, 150.[18]

At the same time, few places had experienced nineteenth-century de-industrialisation as depressingly as Cork city and county.[19] One scholar goes as far as stating that on the eve of the First World War the Cork region 'had reached a low point in its industrial history'.[20] The butter and distilling trades were the primary examples of the economic ebb. Woollen mills, breweries and distilleries still existed in the city and the surrounding towns, but many had closed in the period up to the outbreak of war in 1914. Those remaining were relatively small and dealt largely with local markets, while they experienced increasing competition from their Dublin and Belfast counterparts. After 1890, the area had lost two breweries, five tanneries, four engineering works, a gunpowder plant and many smaller firms.[21] It was not, however, an all-embracing depression. It has been noted that 'certain industries were growing while others were declining'.[22] In the previous centuries, the city had very firmly established itself as a locus of commercial activity for the surrounding regional centres. Cork, as the third largest natural harbour in the world, could still boast one of the world's largest butter markets.

Even though the city had not experienced a full industrial revolution in the nineteenth century there was, as can be seen, some industry, and there were other factors which made it an attractive location for Ford. The proposed location itself was impressive at 136 acres, found on the southern bank of the River Lee, with 1,642 feet of waterfront. A Ford publication published a decade later points out:

> The transport facilities both for export and import are excellent. The proximity of the Great Southern and Western Railway's terminus ensures easy distribution of products throughout the length and breadth of the country, and the river allows vessels up to 10,000 tons to charge and discharge at the Company's wharf.'[23]

It is clear that the selection of the Cork site was due to the favourable conditions for water transportation between the English assembly plant at Manchester (via the Manchester Ship Canal) and later the Ford facilities at Antwerp, Rotterdam, Copenhagen and Stockholm, among others. British-manufactured components could be shipped to Cork for final assembly. It would have held great appeal for Henry Ford to note that the Lee was navigable for ocean-going ships as far as Cork city so that ships of a very large tonnage could unload cargo immediately in front of the main assembly building. Along with this, the land price was also attractive: at '£161.54 per acre, it would compare favourably with the £540.95 paid for Dagenham, even allowing for the seven-year gap between the purchases'.[24]

Cork's port status was undoubtedly a factor in the Ford decision. It is true that the port – even into the second decade of the new century – remained of immense importance to the commerce of the surrounding area.[25] The process of development of the harbour had begun in earnest from the 1820s subsequent to the establishment of the Cork Harbour Commissioners. The work in dredging, bridging, jetty and railway building all facilitated the creeping industry down along the harbour. By these early decades of the twentieth century, the advantages of this facility were widely acknowledged and are demonstrated in an extract from a trade journal dating from 1919:

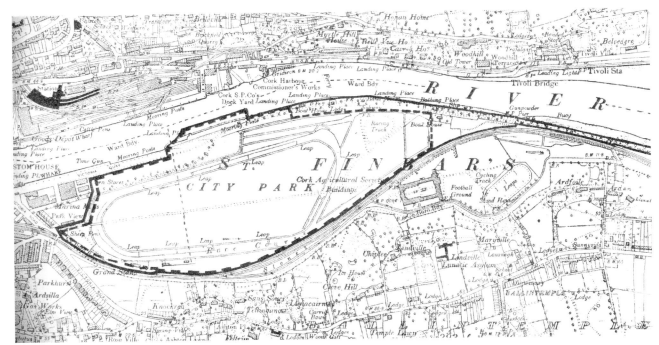

Ordnance Survey map showing proposed Ford site near City Park in 1917.

This is the Cork whose commercial advantages have induced Mr Henry Ford to select it as a suitable site for the development of his celebrated American Motor Works; and whose natural harbour and navigable river caused Messrs. Furniss, Withy & Co. to establish a branch of their shipbuilding works at Passage. This is the Cork, the natural artery for the export of foodstuffs of the rich agricultural hinterland of Munster, whose navigable waterways give access to the wealthy markets of industrial England; and whose large and commodious harbour is the first and most convenient port of call for those gigantic liners rich with the products of the New World.'[26]

In light of this too, it would come as little surprise that the city's economy demonstrated immense interdependence with foreign, and most particularly British trade, confirming the observation that 'development prospects in Ireland were always conditioned, and more often determined, by the political, military, cultural and economic subordination to Britain'.[27]

So, it is vital to point to Cork's role as a nucleus not only for trade, manufacturing and retail but also transport, education, banking, insurance and public administration. The power of the growing Catholic middle class in the early twentieth century took place at the same time that the position of the

Ascendancy was weakening. An ever-growing presence of Catholics in the professions and occupations that had once been a Protestant reserve was the most outward sign of this change. The foundation of the Cork Industrial Association was a tangible sign of the growing confidence of the middle classes.[28] It is possible that Henry Ford would have spotted this expanding cohort as a pool from which future Ford managers and engineers could be drawn.

In terms of how the news of the Ford arrival was received locally, it is important to remember that any self-respecting member of the city's working-class populace would be only too familiar with the impressive changes that Henry Ford's 'five-dollar day' had made to the lot of this class.[29] The Ford firm had doubled American wages in the car industry and sent shockwaves globally.[30] While, it was not the case that wages were exactly matched across the Ford globe, it was noted that in 'all Ford offices around the world employees were beneficiaries of the policy initiated in Detroit'.[31] Yet, the arrival in Cork of the Detroit school of management and work practices would not totally escape criticism. A local trade union publication was quick to point to the anti-union attitudes and policies of the company and would suggest that certain conditions of employment on the Marina were less than desirable.[32] Others lamented the loss of the city race-course.[33]

A factor that made Ireland more attractive than Britain for Ford was the fact that wage rates for the unskilled were substantially lower in Ireland than in the neighbouring island. The largest sector of the workforce hired at Henry Ford & Son Limited at this time was that of unskilled men: they would on average, earn 30 per cent less than they would on contemporary London wage rates.[34] In 1913 the per capita income in Ireland was 57 per cent of Britain's.[35] The wage for labourers in coach building in Ireland was about four-fifths that of England.[36] Soon too, war would drastically stretch British labour demands – most especially when conscription was introduced for all men younger than 41 years, in May 1916. While in contrast, Cork could boast a sizeable and healthy work force, with the added benefit of negligible rivalry from any other large-scale industrial concerns in the region.

The characteristics of the Cork population made it apparent that there would be no shortage of able bodies that would be only too delighted to gain employment in any industrial venture in the area. Henry Ford commented:

> Cork has for many years been a city of casual labour and extreme poverty. There are breweries and distilleries but no real industry. The best that a man could hope for was two

or three days a week on the docks, for which he would receive 60 shillings, or $15, for the hardest kind of stevedoring. If he went out as an agricultural labourer, he could not expect to get more than 30 or 32 shillings a week. None of this work was steady.'[37]

Employment involving the numbers proposed in the Ford factory would clearly be a huge boost to the city's economy. It would be naive to assume that a series of strikes in Manchester's Trafford Park plant in 1912, and into 1913, had no influence on Henry Ford and the other decision makers in consideration of an Irish factory.[38] During this fiasco, Henry Ford was compelled to dispatch one of his closest confidants, Charles Sorenson, from Michigan to resolve the situation. This may have been a matter that would favour Cork over Dublin: most especially in light of the latter city's labour unrest in 1913.[39] Henry Ford's disdain for trade unionism has been well documented and therefore it is difficult to accept that this aspect was not factored into the chosen plant location. It has been suggested that the lack of significant industrialisation, and thus a clearly defined urban working class, meant that trade union radicalism and labour politics had not emerged in Cork to the extent they had in contemporary cities across Europe. One historical study describes the situation:

> Thus, despite some temporary advances labour in Cork by 1911 was, on the surface, in much the same position as it had been twenty years earlier. The railway men were defeated, the dockers were once again without a union to represent them, and the mass of unskilled labourers had gained little or nothing in the way of improved wages and conditions.[40]

The industry in which Henry Ford & Son Limited would establish itself was really only beginning to develop globally at this time. The era of steam-powered tractors was ending with the progress in developing the internal combustion tractor. In fact it seems that the term 'tractor' was actually only used for the first time in the years after 1900 and naturally there is no evidence of tractor manufacture in Ireland at this early stage. Obviously, as a predominantly rural and small island, Ireland did not contribute largely to the lists of vehicle manufacturers extant across Europe at this time. Those who did venture into design and manufacture in Ireland did so in motor vehicles usually, and found the going uniformly tough. With the notable exception of the Belfast based company, Chambers, all disappeared from manufacturing at an early stage.[41]

It was only since the Gordon Bennett Race in 1903 that the general population of Ireland had seen that cars were not to be feared.[42] In a history of the Royal Irish Automobile Club (RIAC) Smith draws attention to the fact that in the latter years of the nineteenth century 'the popularity of automobilism [*sic*] was slow to develop in the Cork/Limerick area. The cult of the horse remained strong and the rail services were still adequate'.[43] Yet, the car was definitely becoming a more common investment as the years of the new century passed. In 1907 the Cork area registered a total of 116 car owners; by 1915 the equivalent figure had risen to 687.[44] In the city area larger carriage building and mechanical engineering firms seemed to gravitate towards the sale and maintenance of motor vehicles – including body building –during the early years of the new century.[45] As early as 1905, Johnson's of Emmet Place offered motor vehicles for hire.[46] By 1912 the city laid claim to twelve carriage-builders and seven motor garages – rising to fourteen carriage-builders and thirteen garages and motor engineers by 1922.[47] There was speedy growth in the number of motor vehicles registered in Ireland from 1905 until the outbreak of the First World War, with more than ten times the numbers of cars on the road by the end of this period.[48]

Cork had a tradition of engineering in shipbuilding and repair, with the Cork Electric Lighting and Power Supply Company, the railways and the Cork Harbour Works.[49] There were several mechanical engineering works where a considerable amount of foundry, mill-wrighting, jobbing, general repair work and manufacture took place.[50] Overall, approximately 1,000 Cork men were employed in these concerns in the city area.[51] But, there was no firm capable of engaging in the repetitive and precise engineering as required for Fords mass production processes and so the company itself would be compelled to manufacture or import all parts. Clearly the methods applied by Fords would require technology not witnessed before in Ireland, or even Europe as a whole. It is important here to recall the fact that this would become the first foreign foundry to be established by the business magnate who historians would soon regard as the pioneer of modern mass production techniques. It would also mark the first Ford factory dedicated solely to the manufacture of tractors.

Overall, the direct effects from four different, but not unrelated, fronts in the political arena, suffocate almost all other considerations in the period between 1914 and 1922: the First World War, the War of Independence, the Civil War and the labour agitation that began in 1917. In a historical account of the Cork economy one scholar described how the ten years following 1914:

> were to fundamentally alter the character and commercial life of the city. There were three main areas of change, the first being in the physical aspect of Cork following the burning of the city centre in 1920. The second was in the attitudes of the majority of businessmen in the city towards belonging to the British Empire and to being under the Crown; they moved from a desire to maintain the status quo to accepting and welcoming – in many cases enthusiastically – a free and independent Ireland. Finally, there was the arrival of the

Fords plant with its modern production line techniques. This was no less dramatic a factor for change in Cork's economy than those already mentioned.[52]

Added to these issues was the fact that contemporary labour unrest saw Cork, from April 1917, experience ongoing strikes. This was primarily the outcome of ever-increasing workers organisation and the unease that roused employers as a result of this politicisation. The constant price increases were also a factor in this working-class discontent.

The geo-political location of Ireland has to be seen as a primary consideration in the decision to set up in Cork.[53] Ireland and Britain were all one jurisdiction under the rule of the British Crown that still prevailed under the 1800 Act of Union. In 1915 the McKenna duties had been put into place, which meant that there was a 33 per cent tariff on imports from areas outside the Empire and a $22^{2/9}$ per cent duty on cars and trucks from within it. This measure was exercised in an effort to gain revenue for war expenses, to discourage the freight of awkward non-essentials and, to some extent, protect British industry. As Ireland was part of the British economy, these duties did not apply, and this must have been a primary concern for Ford. The most significant economic factor was 'the most political of economic factors – tariffs'.[54]

Clearly, from the British viewpoint, the impact of the war situation was, from 1914, becoming increasingly serious.[55] Attacks in British waters by German submarines were having a serious effect on freight. In 1914 the loss was 51,000 tons a month; in 1915, 74,000; and in 1916 it had increased to 103,000 monthly. In February 1917 Germany announced that she would wage unrestricted submarine warfare, and the losses for shipping in March jumped to 310,868 tons: they reached 526,447 in April and continued to rise.[56]

The immediate result of such a campaign was that Britain experienced huge food losses: the country depended on imports for approximately two-thirds of the population's consumption. As the administrative panic set in with more and more meat, sugar and grain destined for the seabed, a resolve to counter the situation was quickly undertaken. Home-grown crops would be free from the threat of submarines and would also free up shipping channels. This very logical idea was put forward, along with many other initiatives that could help the crisis: the use of steam tractors; employing those sent back from the front; and engaging women in the war effort. In the event of the threatened food crisis Henry Ford was called upon to demonstrate his tractor. Impressed with its operation the Ministry of Munitions, under David Lloyd George, was keen to implement its use into the production chain as soon as possible.

Form 178A 2M 12-17

TELEGRAM

Henry Ford & Son. Inc.,

Dearborn, Mich..

Original

Sent: 179 Cablegram Government   February 28th, 1918.   **Via**

Lord Northcliffe

c/o London Daily Mail,
London, (England)

We have shipped to date eighteen hundred assembled tractors and parts for another eighteen hundred knocked down stop   Only ten per cent of this has been loaded aboard ship stop   We have made good time in getting goods to seacoast have sent solid train to Baltimore in four days   Another to Philadelphia in four days stop   Your officials don't get them aboard ship stop   Three thousand tractors laying on the docks don't help food problems anywhere stop   They should all be working the land in thirty days but present facilities and officials at seacoast must be shook up to realize this stop   Canada and this country are begging for these machines stop   Each tractor in England can produce fifty times its weight and bulk this season and in shipping should have preference over food stop   We believe interests or the unseen hand is behind the delay   We suggest that if they cannot be moved in time you release them to us and we will put them to work in Canada and this country

Henry Ford

Box 184 Folder 11 — Tractors - 1918

Cable from Henry Ford to Lord Northcliffe (British war mission) dated 28 February 1918. The details of this communication highlight the urgency with which this matter was being dealt.

Any aspirations held by Henry Ford to start a venture in Ireland depended to some extent on the support of the British administration. At this time, the British government controlled raw materials and shipping, and consequently possessed complete power to facilitate or retard the launch of any new industry.[57] This project with the British government would establish Henry Ford as a vital business and moral ally in the British war effort. This would help counteract some of the negative public opinion in Britain that had surrounded his 'Peace Ship' mission and the hostility that greeted his move into the local motor industry.[58] It is clear that plans were greatly expedited to facilitate the British war effort.[59] During the First World War the Ford Company quickly began to play an important role in the war effort. When presented with an opportunity to develop and produce the machinery that would banish the labour intensive 'drudgery' of agriculture, like any smart businessman, Henry Ford immediately seized his chance to do this at a location that had sentimental attachments for him.[60]

Despite some disadvantages, the Irish economy did possess enough in the realms of communications, banking, wholesale and retail markets, an established administrative system and universal literacy. Geo-politics, genealogical links, global conflict and favourable labour conditions were some of the more notable encouragements that were needed in the Cork bid for the first overseas purpose-built Ford factory. Having looked at the background to the move to Ireland, it is time to turn our attention to the progress made on the Marina in the opening years of the Cork plant.

From a Green Field to a Great Foundry

''Twas [It was] just a large green field with some jumps, of course, and one or two small cottages where the hurling teams used to keep their gear and the rest was a very long riverside frontage to the property, which covered about 150 acres.'
E.L. (Nobby) Clarke, 1982 [1]

'The foundry is the only one of its type in Europe, and has been visited by representatives of firms in Sweden and other foreign countries to study the methods used. There are no secret processes here, all are free to come and learn what they can to the ultimate benefit of purchasers in many different lines of manufactures.'
Ford Times, 1927 [2]

The Cork plant had rapidly made the address 'The Marina, Cork' famous in conversations as near as the Cork suburb of Douglas and as far as Detroit. But, the socio-political setting in Cork was extremely unstable. And so, it is interesting to ponder why, 'despite radical changes in the original fiscal environment which had predisposed the company to manufacture in Ireland, the Ford plant at Cork nevertheless survived'.[3]

The formative years of the Ford works were characterised by a high degree of antagonism, largely caused by external forces. They include the First World War, the domestic conflicts of 1919 to 1923, the economic uncertainty of the newly-formed Irish Free State; and a more specific battle of wills between Henry Ford and Cork's city fathers. Naturally, the resultant effects reverberated in the lives of the employees and those connected with the plant. Exploration of these conflicts will provide a deeper understanding of these crucial years in the Marina's development and should also help to paint a clearer picture of life inside the factory walls.

The building of a modern plant equipped to manufacture and build agricultural machinery was a substantial task in 1917 Cork. To do this, Henry Ford's tractor division head, Charles Sorenson, dispatched a team from the Ford headquarters in the Detroit suburb of Dearborn, who were charged with the exciting assignment.[4] An impressive duty faced the technicians with the need for a machine shop, a foundry, a power house, and an assembly unit on land that was, until then, the location of one of the country's most impressive racecourses and a popular urban park. The site, on the banks of the river Lee, would mark the first foundry in Ford history built on foreign soil and would eventually aim to manufacture an identical unit to the Fordson: production of the tractor had up until then taken place at Dearborn alone.[5]

Cork city's racecourse as it was in 1917, prior to the arrivals of Henry Ford & Son Limited. Note what is now known as the Centre Park Road, running through the centre of the racecourse.

The jumps of Cork city's racecourse in 1917. They were soon to be replaced by a major industrial site.

It has been outlined, during the First World War, the British government's interest in the Fordson tractor presented Henry Ford with the initiative he needed to get his personal project underway. As a result of this, in November 1916, a Southport based businessman named Richard Woodhead had initiated proceedings aimed at the purchase of a 136-acre site in Cork.[6] Finding an agreeable welcome from the city fathers helped matters and an Act of Parliament was subsequently passed to sanction the purchase of this public property.[7] March 1917 saw the British Cabinet announce that, under special licence, Ford would locate in Cork.[8] Negotiations, referred to as those related to 'the Cork Park Project', are documented in local newspapers through February 1917.[9] It was 1 March though before it was confirmed, with the column inches publicising: 'It is announced in the current issue of "Motor Traction" that Messers Henry Ford and Son have received permission from the Government to build works in Cork to make low priced farm tractors'.[10] There had clearly been controversy and jealousies surrounding the decision to use Ford tractors and to locate in Ireland and there is intimation that this was part of a broader effort of Lloyd George to in some way appease Irish sentiments.[11] The organ of the Royal Irish Automobile Club, *Motor News*, provided weekly updates on the arguments as they developed throughout the months of 1917.[12] Rarely does an edition fail to mention this issue in some way.[13] At any rate, plans went ahead and on 17 April 1917 the company of Henry Ford & Son Limited was officially incorporated. By lease dated 27 February 1917 the Cork Corporation demised to Henry Ford & Son Limited the Cork Park lands for a term of 999 years from 9 June 1917 in consideration of a sum of £11,500 and a rent of one penny a year. In addition to the usual covenants, this lease contained obligations that included the spending of £200,000 on construction for industrial purposes within three years; the employment of 2,000 adults at a minimum of one shilling an hour for five years and the building of a road on the leased land.[14] The terms of these undertakings would prove problematic in the future.

The finer details of the events that led to a situation where the British administration would fully support a tractor plant in Cork have been teased out and it has already been seen that the expansion into Ireland was hinged on the global hostilities of 1914 to 1918 that had led to a threatened food shortage in Britain and an ensuing feeling of panic. However, by the time the Marina plant was actually in production, a main driving force for its inception was no longer relevant: the First World War was over. Instead of waiting to use Cork for the much-needed tractor supply, the British government had Henry Ford ship 6,000 tractor units direct from the United States. The net result, however, was that in the founding of the Cork concern Henry Ford had succeeded in establishing a plant to build the machinery that he was most personally interested in, and at that, at a location that formed a focal point of his own identity.

No. *4441*

Certificate of Incorporation.

I hereby Certify That the

Henry Ford & Son Limited

is this day Incorporated under the Companies Acts, 1908 and 1913, and that the Company is Limited.

Given under my hand at Dublin this *Seventeenth* day of *April* One Thousand Nine Hundred and *Seventeen*

Fees and Deed Stamps, £ *30:5/-*
Stamp Duty on Capital, £ *250*

Assistant Registrar of Joint Stock Companies for Ireland.

The Certificate of Incorporation of Henry Ford & Son Limited, dated 17 April 1917.

A view of the waterfront in 1917 prior to any major construction of the new plant.

Excavating the site in 1917. Extensive levelling and pile-driving would be needed before the construction could properly begin.

Meanwhile, construction of the Marina works was fully underway from early summer 1917. The contract was awarded to an Irish firm and at the outset was estimated that it would cost in the region of £300,000.[15] It did however prove more costly and complex than expected 'as the site needed much levelling and pile-driving. The wharves, foundry and machine shop (with a glass roof covering an acre) were built first, then a mobile crane was erected to handle the foundry pig-iron and the wharves were extended. Eventually, the plant covered a floor area of 330,000 square feet'.[16]

Pile-driving in progress using a steam-powered driver with a boiler is visible in the foreground.
Note the stately houses of Montenotte overlooking the construction.

An almost contemporaneous, industrial building with modernist influences was the 'Shannon Scheme' generating station. In fact, Siemens Bau Union erected the transformer station building – to the specification of Siemens-Schuckert, Ltd., Ireland – to house the power transformer equipment supplying current to the factory.[17] With a war ongoing, the building of such an imposing structure as the Marina plant was not always unproblematic. The remarks of the chief engineer of the project highlight the limitations under which construction took place:

The plans for the Cork plant were more or less makeshift. I hired a local engineer. I could get no structural steel or anything of that kind on the regular market. While passing through on a train one day, I saw an old steel structure sticking up in the air. I ascertained the town it was near and sent a man down there to see if it could be bought. That was all the structural steel we used in the building. The rest was all concrete. I secured reinforcing steel from Belgium, and used the old race track grandstand for form lumber. This was after I permitted the Lord Mayor of Cork to have one last horse race at the track before it was torn down. He wanted that last race![18]

A scene which would become familiar on the Marina. Off-loading a ship of supplies onto the Marina for Henry Ford & Son Limited on 24 March 1919.

In spite of the constraints the project was a pioneering example of large structural engineering for the region: the primary significance of the Marina plant architecturally was that its modernist design emanated from the office of the famous Kahn brothers' Detroit office. Henry Ford's favourite architect,

Detroiter Albert Kahn, revolutionised the building of factories and would later influence international architectural stars such as Le Corbsuier, Walter Gropuis and Mier van der Rohe. In fact, the 'Kahn system of reinforced concrete' would make the brothers' name famous in engineering design circles globally and the Kahn-Ford relationship has long been studied.[19]

A 1918 image of the Marina from the opposite side of the river Lee.

With the ground made suitable, the building could begin. Construction of part of the plant, as it looked on 1 June 1918.

The main assembly building, a single-storey unit with partial saw-toothed roof, partial ridged and partial flat-roof, supported on reinforced concrete and exposed steel columns would, when complete, cover 35,500 squared feet.[20] Cork could now boast an example of the most modern industrial architecture and engineering in Europe. The Fordson plant instituted itself on 1 July 1919, with a 44-hour working week.[21] The first tractor came off the line two days later.

The plant as it stood on 22 October 1918. The reinforced concrete and exposed steel columns are clearly visible in this photograph.

The political upheavals of the Cork landscape from the latter years of the second decade of the new century could not but have a bearing on the new Ford works. The city's population was famously republican and it is improbable that some of the personalities involved in the dramatic events had not infiltrated the workforce of Henry Ford & Son Limited.[22] One historian's research has revealed that the Ford plant was 'a hotbed of militant republicanism'.[23] The sizeable Catholic working-class population was to be the primary beneficiary of employment in the construction work and would also form the corpus of the operational labour force. Conversely, the upper echelons of the company's workforce largely came from backgrounds that would be more sympathetic to British interests.[24] The juxtaposition of ideologies that might have existed may have had some impact, but it is also true that this may not have been quite as marked as one would initially suppose. It is essential to remember that the economic

The first Fordson tractor manufactured at Henry Ford & Son Limited. It came off the line on 3 July 1919. Edward Grace, then at the helm on the Marina, is believed to be the individual in the driving seat.

necessity of holding down a job with one of the best-paid employers in the city would, by and large, quell any overly-active political policies or activities within the factory itself. This would be enforced even more so by the Ford company's disdain of overt political participation.

The implications of the War of Independence and the subsequent Civil War fundamentally altered not only the political – but more importantly in Ford's case – the economic position of the market. Fords investment in Cork had been undertaken on the assumption that the fiscal arrangement would continue to exist in the future – flexibility in production was essential so that parts could be manufactured at one plant for assembly at another. All suppositions – under the terms of the subsequently shelved Government of Ireland Act 1914 – were that Ireland and Britain would continue singularly as an economic unit, as far as trade was concerned. Therefore, Ireland would not only retain access to British, but also the other markets of the Empire. When deliberations were initially made in favour of Cork in 1917, it was assumed that this Act would be implemented once the First World War was over. It was only in 1922 that it became clear that this would not be the case. The new position of Ireland economically was a substantive issue. The implication of this situation for the Cork plant would become apparent later.

The political turbulence and violence of the War of Independence and the Civil War in Cork city also affected plant life. The year 1920 in particular demonstrates this harsh reality. Three days after the Cork Lord Mayor Tomas MacCurtain's visit to the Fordson Demonstration, where he was photographed driving a tractor, saw him murdered in his home by several disguised members of the Royal Irish Constabulary.[25] Later in the year, when Terence MacSwiney died on hunger strike, a work stoppage was called in the city to mark his funeral.[26] Trouble arose at the Ford plant. In their invaluable global study of the Ford company, Wilkins and Hill surmised the situation with eloquence:

> How the Ford employees answered a call to midday Mass, supporting the Lord Mayor of Cork, imprisoned and on a hunger strike; how Grace [manager of plant] in anger (he had forbidden them to go) shut down the plant and threatened to hire a new work force, how he relented and reopened the factory, and how Sorenson warned him 'Be careful ... Politics and politicians particularly are things you must be absolutely free and clear of!' are all part of the Irish story.[27]

[Previous page and above] Cork Lord Mayor Tomas MacCurtain's visit to the Fordson Demonstration, 15 March 1920. Three days later he was assassinated by British forces.

Correspondences of American Ford officials to Dearborn provide unique and interesting insights into the situation in Cork. These are not only impressive in how they relate the opinions of somewhat detached observers on the events, but they also emphasise the extraordinary circumstances under which the Cork plant had to almost fight to survive in its infancy. The precarious political circumstances of the city throughout these years were palpable in these reports. As one Ford representative visiting from America detailed in communication:

> Conditions seem to be getting worse instead of better ... it is a nightly occurrence to see armoured cars running around the streets and to hear machine-gunfire all night; the next morning shop windows in the main street can be seen full of bullet holes. My wife and children and myself were held up the other evening whilst we were out for a drive; we were placed under arrest and made to drive to the Barracks between two truckloads of soldiers,

with guns pointing all around us, but we got off all right without serious mishap.[28]

Similarly, on the occasion of the December 1920 burning of the city by the Auxiliaries and the Black and Tans, Edward Grace (the American who was at the helm of the Cork works), relayed a compelling breakdown of the events to Dearborn. This correspondence makes fascinating reading, especially when it is noted that the summary is provided by a somewhat neutral observer of the events.

It is unfortunate that the ending of the War of Independence could not herald a period of peace for the country. The violence continued right through 1922 and into 1923 and probably the most famous casualty of this ugly period of Irish history was Michael Collins who was assassinated in August 1922. He too had visited the Fordson plant, just months prior to his untimely death.

The production of tractors at the Marina continued, nevertheless, in spite of the surrounding turmoil.[29] From August 1921 the factory's impressive foundry had also begun to produce all the Manchester plant's cast-iron necessities. The workforce hovered in and around 1,000 employees during these initial years. An update from Edward Grace to the city's Lord Mayor in August 1921 is instructive in detailing the achievements of the plant to date and surveying conditions of the workplace more generally:

> We have … in spite of the most formidable difficulties due in the first instance to the war and the after-war restrictions, and in the second to the hostilities in this country – erected buildings which cover over six acres of ground at a cost of approximately half a million … Last January we had 1,500 men on our payroll and, unfortunately, just at the moment when our Cork factory was able to commence production on a large scale a serious slump took place in the motor trade everywhere, and due to these circumstances work had to be restricted here also and the staff reduced. Things are now improving, however, and at the present moment our firm has 940 men employed, who are paid at the rate of 2/1 per hour, or more – or double the wages stipulated for in the lease. I need scarcely say that having expended such large sums in buildings and plant at Cork it is in our own interest to employ as many men as possible to make our expenditure of capital productive, and that it is our intention to do so. I may mention that our expenditure in wages alone since we came to Cork amounts to £425,000.[30]

DIRECTORS
E. B. FORD
C. E. SORENSEN
E. G. LIEBOLD
EDW. GRACE
W. C. ANDERSON

E. L. CLARKE

UNITED STATES.

TELEGRAMS: & CABLES
FORDSON, CORK
TELEPHONES
CORK. 1045
1046
1047

Henry Ford & Son, Ltd.

Cork, Ireland.

MANUFACTURERS OF

Fordson
FARM TRACTORS.

Mr. C. E. Sorensen,
Ford Motor Company,
River Rouge Plant,
Dearborn,
Michigan, U. S. A.

Dept. 2

December 17th, 1920.

ALL STATEMENTS OR AGREEMENTS CONTAINED IN THIS LETTER ARE CONTINGENT ON STRIKES ACCIDENTS FIRES, OR ANY OTHER CAUSES BEYOND OUR CONTROL AND ALL CONTRACTS ARE SUBJECT TO APPROVAL BY THE SIGNATURE OF A DULY AUTHORIZED EXECUTIVE OFFICER OF THIS COMPANY. CLERICAL ERRORS SUBJECT TO CORRECTION.

My dear Mr. Sorensen:

Following your cablegram and request that I
report on the condition of the fire in Cork, I am mailing you photo-
graphs of the scene taken on Sunday morning while the ruins were
still burning, also copy of the "Cork Weekly Examiner" which gives
a very thorough, full report, as well as the "Cork Weekly News."

In my cable I mentioned that the Auxiliary
Police and Black and Tans were alleged to be responsible for the
burning of this large portion of the business district of Cork.
Patrick Street is the main thoroughfare of the City in which is
situated all of the chief shops, and several hundred families
have been rendered homeless, who were residing in the upper stories
of the business houses.

There seems to be little room left in the
minds of the general public for doubt as to whom are guilty of the
burning and looting of this district. In order to explain who
the Auxiliary Police and Black and Tans are I wish to point out
that up to the present time there have been four separate and
distinct bodies in Ireland. First, There is the old R. I. C. -
Royal Irish Constabulary - which is the ordinary old police force,
and is composed of men, the greater number of whom are sound dis-
ciplined men. Second, the military who are here in thousands
fully equipped with armoured cars, tanks, and all modern implements
of war, such as machine guns, automatic pistols, etc: Third, the
Black and Tans, so called because of their wearing part soldiers'
uniform and part police uniform. These are a band of men sent
over from England and seem to be without any proper discipline.
They have not been under the control of either the military or
police, but seem to carry on as they please without respect to
any common decency. They have been alleged to have held up people
to search them for political documents, and in every instance where
a man had money on him they have relieved him of it. I have,
fortunately not had any encounter with any of them, but, judging

from/

Henry Ford & Son, Ltd.
Cork, Ireland

from the appearance of their faces, would say that they are a lot of the scum of England who have accepted the high pay offered them to come here to do police duty, and are spending the same on booze – that is when they are not able to steal it.   The Auxiliary Police is a body composed of ex army officers recruited in England, and, while they are perhaps a little better type of men than the Black and Tans, seem to be uncontrolled and allowed to do as they please. The burning of Cork is alleged to have been caused directly by a lorry full of Auxiliary Police having been fired upon and 16 of them wounded and one of them killed last Saturday evening, after which they all went mad and sought to destroy the City as a reprisal. As much as all sane thinking people deplore the act of cowardly murdering men from ambush, still, one cannot imagine a modern Government allowing its armed forces to take part in such an orgy of crime.

Following all this, on Saturday night an order has been issued placing Cork district under Martial Law, which means that all armed forces will be under direct command of the Commanding Military Officer in the district, and while people are deprived of a great many privileges because of Martial Law, still, apparently everyone is satisfied, because, at least, they know that the City is under the command of an organization which has always been under strictest discipline, and I am sure that no further acts of this nature will be committed again.

As far as the Works is concerned we are in no danger: firstly, because it is owned by an American, and they fear that it might involve international complications, and next because we have about 1,500 men employed, and while so employed they have no time to think of other matters than their work.   The only portions of our buildings that they could do any real damage to through fire are the wooden buildings, which are covered well by Insurance.   I have been assured by the officer in charge here that we need have no fear from anything of this nature in the future.

Yours faithfully,

EG*NH

HENRY FORD & SON, LIMITED.

A fascinating account from Henry Ford & Son Limited to headquarters at Dearborn, reporting on the burning of Cork in December 1920. That this was penned by a somewhat neutral observer only adds to its authenticity.

ADDRESS OFFICIAL COMMUNICATIONS TO
THE SECRETARY OF STATE
WASHINGTON, D. C.

DEPARTMENT OF STATE
WASHINGTON

August 4, 1922.

In reply refer to
2A 012-3-Ford Motor.

Ford Motor Company,

    River Rouge, Michigan.

Gentlemen: Attention Mr. Sorensen.

    The Department has received from the American
Consul at Dublin a cable message dated August 2,
4 p.m., 1922, communicating the following message
to you from "Grace Manager Ford Motor Works". The
telegram is sent in paraphrase, as follows:

    "QUOTE. Send me in plain English via
    Commercial a strong cablegram ordering me
    to close plant entirely if any troops inter-
    fere too much. The rebels have conscripted
    some of our men. In my opinion, we will not
    be troubled further if you send such message.
    If you think the matter should be handled
    confidentially cable through State Depart-
    ment to Queenstown Consulate. Will not close
    plant. UNQUOTE."

I am, Gentlemen,

    Your obedient servant,

        For the Secretary of State:

        Assistant Secretary.

*Cable to Dearborn from Henry Ford & Son Limited, 4 August 1922. This correspondence gives an indication of the precarious
position in which the plant was operating at the time.*

Fires still raging on St. Patrick's Street after the burning of Cork, December 1920.

A tram passing the burnt out shell of City Hall, February 24th, 1921.

People searching through the rubble on St. Patrick's Street.

Spectators observe the ruins of buildings on St. Patrick's Street.

Locals attempt to quench the fire.

{Above and overleaf} Views of a devastated St. Patrick's Street.

A man works on a fire-damaged building on what is now known as Oliver Plunkett Street (then King's Street).

A man works on a fire-damaged building on St. Patrick's Street.

The temporary power house in 1921 where dynamos are powered by Fordson tractors during a strike in the local power house.

Looming, however, was a weighty threat to the future of Ford activity in Ireland. This foe came under the guise of Cork Corporation. The disharmony had started during 1921 regarding the building of the road, as mentioned in the lease. Eventually, in November of that year, agreement was reached and the company undertook the construction of a road across the centre of the land.[31] This was not where the matter ended though. In spring of 1922 the Corporation passed a motion to serve notice on Henry Ford & Son Limited that called on them to comply with the covenant of the lease regarding the employment of 2,000 men. Having seen reports of this in the American press, Henry Ford immediately cabled Grace to close the plant and remove the business elsewhere unless the outstanding compulsions in the lease were waived. In this action, the Ford entity was making no idle threat:

> We duly received your cable regarding the cutting down of all construction and installation work, and as from yesterday we cut our forces down by 329 men. This number no doubt will be increased from day to day, as we are only going to have production work around here and the bearest [*sic.*] amount of maintenance labour, until the Corporation show some better common sense.[32]

The stand off between both parties led to a tense period for the city: all watched with bated breath. Newspapers, both local and national, provided daily commentary on the impasse.[33] No doubt, influenced by the utterly instantaneous and resolute response of Henry Ford, the city administration withdrew the notice served ten days previously, on 10 March 1922, and authorised the city solicitor to enter into negotiations with the company with a view to an amicable settlement. This was duly reached.

The reasons as to why this distasteful episode occurred is questionable when it is considered that the plant was employing 1,600 men at a wage of 2/1 per hour and paying over £8,000 a week in wages; whereas the weekly wages of 2,000 men at 1/- an hour, under the lease covenant, would only have amounted to £4,800. Grace's explanatory comments to Dearborn on this issue are of interest:

> However, the one thing I wish to ask you to look over is the apparent antagonism of some members of the Corporation. If you fully understood the conditions here and knew under what circumstances the Corporation was elected, you could make allowance for the action of some of the members. The present Corporation is not a representative body, and when things settle down here, we will have a better set of men to run the city.[34]

The incident illustrates a resolve of Henry Ford that he advocated in his business practices: to remove himself from overt political considerations as much as was possibly viable and to assert the lone motivation of any Ford concern as being those of the dictates of trade. The following extract from a letter from Henry Ford to Grace on the issue reflects this:

> Make no changes in your plans and operations whatever. We stand ready to go and will
> do so immediately on their order without protest ... Further we will go no further under
> any restrictions of this lease. If this lease is not removed at once we will proceed to move
> to other localities where we are not handicapped.[35]

Throughout and immediately following the Corporation controversy, it became all too clear that the slump in demand for tractors, the protectionist nature of export markets and the establishment of the Irish Free State – and its intrinsic implications – meant that serious and swift modifications of production were needed at the Marina works.[36] The fact that it was cheaper to manufacture and ship tractors direct from Dearborn led to a situation where it was decided to cease production and on 'December 29, Fordson No. 253,562, the 7,605[th] Cork-built tractor, came off the line'.[37] The harsh reality of the 22 per cent duty, that was now due on parts for Manchester from April 1923, also meant that the fabrication of Model T parts was no longer economically viable. Manufacture of parts for Britain would continue: but only until a suitable site was located and established in England. In the interim, Cork would maintain its production for the neighbouring demand and also handle the requirements of the domestic market. This was an industrious time for Cork and is reflected by the fact that on 31 July 1923 the payroll was numbered at 1,850 employees.[38] It was estimated that Henry Ford & Son Limited provided employment to at least 15 per cent of Cork's breadwinners.[39]

A fleet of 25 new Motel Ts for the Irish Army at the Marina in 1927, priced at £150 each.

On the production front, the plant was continuing to manufacture and assemble the Model T, with 1927 marking the year of the final example of the 'Universal Car' coming off the line. The Cork plant was now under the stewardship of the first native Irish manager when the Sligo man, E.L. (Nobby) Clarke had replaced Edward Grace in the summer of 1926. The cessation of the Model T would lead to a period of unprecedented activity in Cork. Not only would production and assembly of the Model A and AF now take place at the Irish works but with the closure of the Dearborn tractor facility, it was decided that Cork would revert to its former role. The Marina would accommodate the only Ford tractor manufacture facility in the world.[40] The duality of production would see the payroll temporarily explode up to around 7,000 in the late 1920s.[41] Cork's eminence was bolstered by the foundry's very formidable reputation.[42] As Clarke tells:

> we had a great foundry in Cork, a wonderful foundry, we had five cupolas melting iron. We could melt up to 150 tonnes of metal in the day and we had wonderful core makers and ... men of the various operations required in a foundry ... It was considered one of the most modern foundries in Europe. And we had foundry managers come not only, from England, but from other European companies to see the methods adopted by Ford, because they were ... a repeat of what was happening in the United States.[43]

In the intervening years, it is understandable that the internal dynamics of the Cork works had developed the expected characteristics of a factory. The newly-found peace in the city provided the Ford workers with an environment that could be more conducive to the normalities of working life. This situation lent itself to the natural development of interaction and activities that went beyond the necessities of the relationships of the working day. An early and illustrious example of this progression towards a sense of a Ford community was manifested by the Fordson football team's win of the 1926 Free State Cup.[44] Only four years after their inception, this factory team had achieved a unique victory by beating the reigning champions, Shamrock Rovers. One review of the newspapers' coverage of this event recounts descriptions of the thousands of Fordson fans who had made the journey from the Glanmire terminus to Dublin's Dalymount Park on St Patrick's Day 1926 and the celebrations to mark the victory:

> Extraordinary scenes of excitement were witnessed in Cork when the victorious team came home the following night. For hours before they were due, huge crowds began to converge on the station and its environs. When the train steamed in at 9.40pm, the station yard was crammed; so also was the Lower Road back as far as St Patrick's ... All traffic was stopped for the massive procession, headed by the Parnell Guards Band which,

with the Working Men's Band, played them through the streets lined with applauding crowds. St. Patrick's Street was also packed with men, women and even children from footpath to footpath and wave after wave of thunderous cheering broke out as the heroes entered the Victoria Hotel.[45]

The Ford workforce in 1926.

There is little doubt that even in the plant's short existence in the city it was fundamentally improving the lives of those connected with it. Working conditions at the Marina were the most progressive and benevolent in the region and this, coupled with the impressive wage rates, meant that Fords rapidly became the pre-eminent employer. As one of the leading engineers asserted: 'When Mr Ford established a shilling-an-hour wage scale, the local Irishman could hardly believe his ears. He figured there just *must* be some trick involved. They had never heard of such a wage scale before.'[46] Henry Ford himself reflected on his company's impact on the pre- and post-Ford Cork workforce just a few years later, in one of his ghost-written works. Here he is quoted as remarking:

The men and their families did not really live. They had no homes – only hovels. No clothing but what they had on. We started our plant with three men from Detroit to direct operations. Now we have under regular employment about 1800 men. They work eight hours a day, five days a week – steadily. The minimum wage is two shillings and sixpence per hour, or a sovereign a day – five pounds a week. This is steady money, week in and week out – something that few, if any, of the men had ever before known. We have no labour turnover whatsoever, and always have a long waiting list.[47]

Named after the vehicle they were producing, Ford's football team, The Fordson's won the Free State Cup in 1926

The arrival of Fords in Ireland meant that, for the first time, the most modern of motor vehicle – and for a while too agricultural machinery – production techniques were being carried out on Irish soil. As late as 1913 the Ford Motor Company had made a massive impact on automotive manufacture by pioneering the modern moving assembly line at the Highland Park Plant in Michigan. More locally, as Nobby Clarke would recall in interview: 'I suppose the great thing is to really understand how well Cork integrated itself into that sort of production movement, of engineering and assembling, at the best and highest standards.'[48] This would mark a meaningful departure in the engineering history of the newly-formed state.

The Fordson's Team, who were Munster Senior Cup and League winners in 1929.

A 1920s photograph of some of the senior management on the Marina. Edward Grace (managing director) is fourth from the left and his successor, E.L. (Nobby) Clarke, is second from the left whilst Ernest Blythe (minister in the Free State government) is second from the left.

When Dubliners boasted the brewing excellence as exemplified by Guinness, and Northerners proudly laid claim to Harland and Wolff, Cork now too claimed its own important location on the Irish industrial map. And what's more is that the optimism, for what lay ahead, was being reiterated by the company's founding father:

> He [Henry Ford] told me that the output of the Cork plant will be increased to 300 tractors daily, and said there was no reason why half the world's supply of tractors should not be made in Cork.[49]

Cork Ford workers spill out of the plant in the early 1920s.

Picture the spectacle of 7,000 men and women converging on 'Ford's Road' in early morning and the subsequent outpouring at the end of each working day. Visualise the impact of the injection of Ford pay packets into the city's economy on a weekly basis. In early 1929 the wage bill on the Marina amounted to about £2,000 daily.[50]

It can only have been striking in a city that had never before seen such large-scale employment under the roof of one concern. Detractors disapproved of and criticised the newly-found dependency on the

Ford facility.[51] In spite of this, waiting lists for employment at the Marina consistently lengthened. A position in the plant had swiftly become a hallmark of upward mobility and security for employees. In the space of a decade, the site had been transformed from 'a large green field with some jumps' to one of the major industrial sites in the Irish Free State and marked an early European example of the concept in practice that was coined as 'Fordism'.

An adverfisment highlighting the contribution of Ford to Cork. Cork Examiner, 22 May 1930.

Meanwhile, in the preceding years Henry Ford had been busily concentrating on developing his world-renowned River Rouge plant in Michigan. A 2,000-acre site close to the Rouge River was secured in July 1915 that would eventually play host to one of the great industrial feats of the world and would employ over 100,000 workers. It was time to turn his attention eastwards and review the situation in Europe.

A 1919 photograph of one of the early Ford dealerships in Ireland: Sheridans Garage in Waterford city.

Another 1919 photograph of the range of Ford vehicles carried by Sheridans.

As outlined earlier, the need for change became even more urgent when the new political status of Ireland was clear after the signing of the Treaty in December 1921 and the economic impact that this would have on the manufacture of parts for Britain. Yet, the formation of the Irish Free State was not the major catalyst that would stimulate the huge expansion that subsequently developed in Britain. Land purchases had been made by the company in the Southampton area as far back as 1915 and 1916.[52] There does, however, seem to have been a lethargic attitude regarding any substantial expansion into Britain, until the realities of the tariffs between Ireland and her nearest neighbour became apparent. The future of the Cork plant would quickly need to be reassessed along with the consideration of the provision of engines and castings for the Manchester plant.[53] It is important to remember that at this time the Irish plant was one of the larger operations. Wilkins and Hill provided data in their study:

> In late 1923, of the European Ford establishments, Manchester towered above the others with assets of $14.8 million and a work force of 2,580. Cork, with $7.3 million assets and 1850 employees, ranked second. Next came Denmark, with resources of $6.8 million and 390 workers, and there followed France, Spain and the new companies in Belgium and Italy, all with smaller capital, property and number of workers.[54]

A site was purchased twelve miles southeast of London at Dagenham in Essex in 1924. However, this action did not immediately sound the death knell for the Cork concern. As a result of the English Finance Act of 1921, the Ford Model T was uncompetitive in comparison with other vehicles on the British market. Henry, staunch in his loyalty to the car that had ensured his legendary status, refused to alter the design, so as to minimise the impact that this horsepower tax would have. There would be no new car produced for the English requirement, so that the Dagenham site would remain idle for some years. Cork, meanwhile, would continue manufacturing parts for Manchester. In 1927, the Marina was exporting over £400,000 of parts annually.[55]

As a result of the British car tax situation and the mounting concern over car sales worldwide, again, it seems that Henry's attention was diverted away from the specifics of expansion in England. It had become clear that a new Ford model was required to compete in the changing markets. The job of replacing the Model T would be of pivotal importance for Henry Ford, on many different levels. This was the vehicle that had made him a very wealthy and influential figure globally. Also, one needs to remember the colossal impact that this vehicle and its manufacture had in terms of the wider implications for transport and movement of people, as well as the influences in the spheres of work practices and industrial relations. As

Walter Reuther, former Ford employee and later president of the United Automobile Workers, remarked:

Only after Henry Ford showed the rest of them how did industry begin to build for the large number of consumers. He structured the idea of the mass market which required mass production which made it possible to utilise the advance technology that science was beginning to furnish at that time ... He combined his personal mechanical genius with a unique understanding of this basic fact – mass consumption makes mass production possible.[56]

One of the first Model As to reach Europe being loaded on to the SS Ardmore *to Liverpool on 3 January 1928. T.D. Murdoch, manager of the City of Cork Steam Packet Company, and J. O'Callaghan, Quay Superintendent, oversee the operation.*

The success of the Model T was the cornerstone in the foundations of the Ford Motor Company as it existed by this time. It really was the 'jewel in the crown'. But, nineteen years and many millions of cars later, it was time for a change.[57] However, a heavy burden weighed on any successor to the famous Model T. Expectation would naturally abound. It was late in 1927 when the Model A hit newspaper headlines and with this task complete Henry could now refocus on his strategy in Britain.[58] This was to have major implications for the Cork plant.

A Ford Model Y 'Baby Ford' parked outside a dealership on Cork's MacCurtain Street in the 1930s.

The Dagenham Yanks

'Most countries sent out oil or iron, steel or gold to somewhere else but Ireland had only one export – her people'
John F. Kennedy, 1963[1]

'People can get "lost" for all sorts of reasons, not least because the material which might have allowed us to hear their voices, and which might have allowed us to study them, has not survived.'
Patrick O'Sullivan, 1992[2]

One recalls that Henry's 1912 visit to Europe had provided an impetus that lead to the formation of the plant in Cork. In a similar fashion, a trip to England in April 1928 would have important knock-on effects on Cork's future. This was clearly a fact-finding mission and it demonstrated his enthusiasm for a more dominant profile for the Ford brand name in European territories.[3] The requisites for Henry's ambitious new plan for Dagenham were now being put in place, and the operation would be headed up by the person who had been instrumental in introducing the Ford name into Britain and Ireland in the pre First World War period: Sir Pervical Perry. The framework that would facilitate this large European development, by mirroring the American model, became known as the '1928 plan'.[4] This meant that the large manufacturing plant would be centralised at Dagenham, while the Manchester site would revert to existence as an assembly location and Cork would reinvent itself in its original role as a tractor-producing facility.

As a result of these wider plans, Cork soon saw shipments of manufacturing machinery roll into her harbour from November 1928.[5] As had occurred in the previous decade, American expertise was dispatched to oversee the new operation and manufacture at the Marina. It is important to recollect that with the Dearborn tractor factory now closed, Cork resumed an esteemed position in the Ford global community as the only tractor factory within the company. This function saw the Leeside facility export tractors to locations spanning all continents and also the fulfilment of a mammoth parts order for Russia. Meanwhile, construction of the Dagenham plant was underway from May the following year. It seemed that nothing could go wrong. Even the stock market crash on Wall Street in October 1929 failed, for the time being, to dampen spirits in either Dearborn or Cork. According to Wilkins and Hill:

> The early months of 1930 seemed to proclaim that the boom would continue indefinitely. At Cork the tractor plant had more orders than it could fill and in February alone assembled 3,026 machines. The foundry hummed with full-time activity making Fordson parts and castings for Ford-England. The plant now employed 7,000 men

(Manchester used only 2,600) and was the largest employer of labour throughout the Ford overseas empire. Aside from the railroads, it used more workers than any other company in the Irish Free State.[6]

Despite the hectic nature of business, the Cork plant also had time to maintain a reputation for cleanliness and order:

> The main thing that strikes one about this whole factory, both in the foundry and the machine shops, is the unusual cleanliness of the floors, etc. There are few foundries into which one cares to take a lady on account of the dust and dirt; but there is no fear of anyone's clothes, however delicate, receiving injury in walking through these shops in Cork.[7]

A Fordson tractor being put to the test on the Ford farm at the Marina.

History shows explicitly that the launch of Dagenham – the 'Detroit of Europe' – in 1928 could not have been initiated at a worse time in the economic history of the twentieth century. It was not too long before the impact of the American Smoot-Hawley tariff in June 1930 would make its presence known, along with the wider implications of protectionism within the world economies in the early 1930s. If the suddenness of the upsurge that had hit the Cork factory in recent years had caught those involved by surprise, likewise, the rapidity with which the depression was felt was most palpable. Production figures for these years are probably the most effective means of demonstrating the spectacularly abrupt nature of the rise and fall of tractor demand. 1929 produced 9,686 units, 1930 produced 15,196 units, 1931 produced 3,501 units and 1932 produced 3,088.[8]

The unanticipated slump meant that in the months of May and June 1930 almost 6,000 employees were laid off from the Marina plant.[9] Obviously, in a city the size of Cork, this level of unemployment was devastating to the local economy. It was becoming clearer that there were frugal times on the horizon. Ford management in Britain and America needed to react promptly to Ireland's weakening sales position and to the imposition of even more tariff barriers with Britain. Soon it was decided that the Cork plant would relinquish its tractor fabrication department and return to assembly exclusively.

For the second time in Henry Ford & Son Limited's brief history, in July 1932, after a four-year term of office, tractor manufacture was terminated. In total, 39,049 tractors had been assembled in Cork.[10] Dagenham's gain was Cork's loss and this sealed the fate of those who would soon become known as the 'Dagenham Yanks'. This sequence of events, combined with the depressed nature of the Irish economy, meant that the new Ford location in Essex would become a beacon of employment for Cork men. Meanwhile, any excitement that should have surrounded the launch of the new Model Y and the even more consequential opening of Europe's sophisticated new outfit was undoubtedly dampened by the economic downturn in 1932. Nevertheless, the Ford-Britain outfit quickly assumed its position directing the plants in Ireland, Belgium, Holland, Spain, Turkey, and the Scandinavian countries – as well as sales companies in Portugal, Romania, Greece, Italy and Egypt. The Dagenham plant produced its first truck at 2pm on 1 October 1931, but full production only began towards the end of the summer the following year. By the end of 1932, the workforce was at 7,024, with 2,000 of these having been brought in from the plants in Cork and Manchester.

It made good business sense to bring not only the heavy machinery that was necessary in the manufacture of tractors to the new location from Cork, but also the highly skilled labour that now existed at Henry Ford and Son Limited.[11] As records of the actual numbers of people who would have moved in this fashion are unavailable, it is difficult to precisely assess the actual impact that Cork men would have made on the floor of the new Ford facility. However, the following 1954 commentary does provide some indication of how many may have been involved in the move to Essex: 'Of particular Irish interest is the Ford Foundry, where 50 per cent of the 3,300 men are Irish: our proportion in the supervisory grades – men with fifteen to twenty years experience at Dagenham – is even higher.'[12] Clearly, this description pertains to the wider Irish community, rather than specifically the Cork employees in the foundry – which itself was only one part of this impressive site. Over time, there is no doubt that some employees would have hailed from places outside Cork city and that some of those hired would not have had previous experience working in the Marina plant. Yet, all indications would be that in the initial wave of migration to Essex the majority involved were indeed Cork men who had worked previously at the Leeside factory.

The establishment of this massive new plant saw the emergence of a pattern of labour migration that would last a considerable period and saw Dagenham very firmly establish itself as a major employment zone for migrants from the Munster capital. And so, it is helpful to look at these migrants in a broader context, since there was a tradition of transience from Cork to the Greater London area. Migration remained a strong feature of Irish life following the formation of the Irish Free State and it remained so for some time. The dominance of this demographic feature was marked in southern counties since the famine years. Between 1946 and 1951 Cork and Kerry featured prominently in the six counties that accounted for over 55 per cent of the net migration volume. Cork, as the country's largest county, naturally topped the list.[13] The poor economic performance of the 1920s was compounded by the events surrounding the depressed years of the following decade. When a concern, such as that of Henry Ford & Son Limited, laid off employees as it did in the early 1930s and then announced the opening of the plant at Dagenham shortly afterwards, it was natural that some would emigrate in pursuit of employment to the neighbouring island.

Regarding migratory destination, it was during the 1930s that Britain reclaimed the position as the most popular stop for the Irish migrant.[14] From the Famine until this time the United States had become home for about 75 per cent of Irish migrants.[15] Now, a new trend in migration could be seen. Prior to this, by and large, migrants rarely returned to Ireland for any extended period of time. The lack of geographical proximity dictated this in a world that, as yet, knew little of modern transport and communication methods. The relative closeness and accessibility of was an obvious part of the appeal for Cork people and would fit into a long tradition of Irish migration to the major industrial centres of Britain. Areas such as Manchester, Glasgow, Leeds, Birmingham and Lancashire all possessed well-established Irish communities of their own – as did London and its environs.

From 1932 onwards thousands of Cork men travelled to gain employment in the new Ford Motor Company site at Dagenham and later at other Ford locations, such as Leamington Spa, Manchester and Basildon. The sobriquet 'Dagenham Yank' was loosely applied to those who may or may not have actually worked at the Essex concern; generally people at home in Cork did not distinguish between the locations; once a person migrated to work for Ford they could always be labelled a 'Dagenham Yank'. The sequence of movement between Cork and the English Ford sites varied. There seems to have been a large-scale wave of those who moved over and settled in Dagenham, Barking, Romford and surrounding areas on an almost permanent basis. Mostly, these men secured long-term positions and had little, if anything, to do with the Cork facility. Simultaneously, there was a consistent trajectory of transitory migration between the Marina and England. A lull in production in Cork would promptly see the movement of individuals across the Irish Sea, where obviously they would be offered slightly preferential treatment as existing Ford employees.[16] These periods in England would often be short and it was not uncommon for Cork workers to partake in numerous stints working for the company in the neighbouring country.[17] This migration pattern draws many parallels with the seasonal migrants from Killybegs and Dungloe who travelled for sugar-beet work in England and Scotland from September to February.[18]

But why did people go? What were the 'push' and 'pull' factors that motivated the decision-making process? At the outset, the primary determinant was economic. The economic stagnation of Ireland in this period and the lack of employment were critical. With the opening of the plant at Dagenham came a much-welcomed opportunity for the employment of men from Cork. Jobs were a scarce commodity all round in the decades prior to and following the Second World War. For many the decision made at this time was one of necessity as households needed income and children needed to be fed. There was little employment in the city and the prospects for the future were none too encouraging either. As the migration historian, Enda Delaney, points out, these 'emigrants left in order to earn a livelihood which was not available in Ireland; perceived better opportunities in Britain, unemployment in Ireland and the general economic malaise are more plausible explanations of the emigrant's decision to travel to Britain'.[19] The centrality of economics is highlighted by the comment of the son of a Dagenham Yank:

> I can remember my mother waiting for the telegram to come … with the money in it, every week.[20]

And so, a decision was made. For some it was easier than others. It is inaccurate to assume that for all or even any considerable group the move 'to Britain was often the result of a sudden impulse. A week's wages would pay the way over, and if things did not work out, another week's wages would pay the way home again.'[21] A sizeable proportion of those considering emigration would have been married and may already have had their own families. Some of these men would have gone alone and the families would have followed at a later stage. Other men travelled unaccompanied and remained without their spouses and families for extended periods of time. The variances in how certain people integrated and assimilated into life in a new country are fascinating and manifold. Some never fully settled whilst others did. By and large, economic constraints meant that far more Cork families did put down roots and make their homes in England rather than return to Cork.

The departure of the *Innisfallen* from Penrose Quay bound for Fishguard became an established routine for the city's labour force.

Aerial view of the Marina in the 1960s. Note the Inisfallen *docked at Penrose Quay (Centre right).*

Most families or extended families had at least one member ensconced in what became known in the Cork inflection as 'Dagnum'. Remittances were eagerly awaited and the fact that in the late 1940s and early 1950s there were up to 40 telegram boys delivering – for the most part telegraph money orders – around the city gives some indication of the economic importance of the workers in Britain for many dependents.[22] It is speculated that between 1939 and 1969 in the region of £3 billion in postal money orders and cheques were returned from Britain.[23] A boy who at seventeen followed his father to work in Dagenham recalled his circumstances:

> I was able to send home … £5 a fortnight, you see, to my mother. There were five siblings at home … that means…I was earning about £5 a week where … I'd say the wages here in Cork would have been about £2 a week – a married man might have been earning £2 a week.[24]

During the Second World War in particular, Irish wage levels had fallen considerably behind those of Britain. A comparison of industry-wide levels in 1938 and 1946 suggest that the gap between Irish and British men's wages rose from 16 to 32 per cent, while that of women rose from 8 to 31 per cent.[25]

A number of wives in Cork did not want to leave their homes and extended families in the area. Subsequently, hundreds of homes in the city were fatherless and led to a situation where there was a substantial core of single-parented families. A Mayo migrant, John Healy, described these as the women who survived 'with a two-month-of-the-year marriage and the loneliness of life without a husband or father'.[26] Thus, over a couple of generations, while Cork experienced a situation where a portion of the city's homes were run solely by women, there were thousands of children who only knew their fathers by weekend return trips or a summer-holiday stay. Understandably, instances of dual families would be another legacy for men who had made the move to England alone or spent long periods living in isolation from familial ties, although this was the exception rather than the norm. One Cork informant recalled in interview:

> … they'd be waiting for their father to come home and he wouldn't come…They'd even be down at the boat to meet them and they wouldn't arrive, so they were kind of sad things as well.[27]

Probably one of the most enduring narratives surrounding the 'Dagenham Yanks' is that which recalls their return trips to the city so many of them had left. The description represents a part of the lore of Cork and is indisputably the most common means by which these migrants are remembered, even today.

According to these recollections the 'Dagenham Yank' typically donned the most fashionable of suits while boasting of 'their "big" money' in the city's pubs for the two-week duration of the trip home to Cork.[28] Tales of their running out of money before the end of their holiday and slipping in and out of the newly-acquired English accent serve as reminders of the ambivalence with which the returned emigrants have historically been viewed in Irish society. Referring specifically to the Dagenham Yanks, the oral testimony of one Cork man revealingly commented: 'You'd think they were coming from a different planet, you know, and they probably were'.[29]

The beginning of hostilities in 1939 is deemed as a 'turning point in Irish emigration' and certainly had huge consequences on the Ford enterprises in both Ireland and Britain'.[30] The Ford enterprise and the role of the Irish diaspora are an inherently intertwined example of the importance of Irish labour during the conflict. Just as Henry Ford had assisted during the First World War, the establishment of the Leamington Spa plant was a direct outcome of the war effort, where the first vehicle came off the assembly line in February 1942.[31] With the dire need for labour in Britain and the constantly rising unemployment figures in Ireland, it is hardly surprising that thousands of Cork men spent time working at locations such as this, especially after June of the same year, when production ceased at the Marina site.[32] The well-established migration path that existed between Cork and Dagenham under the auspices of the Ford company must have made the route a little easier for those who found themselves boarding the boat on the Cork quays. The lines of a letter from Henry Ford & Son Limited's manager to the Office of the Minister for Industry and Commerce outline some of the measures that were taken in this direction:

> 'At our request the Ford Motor Company, England, have agreed to accept for employment at their various phases of activity any number up to 500 of our men, provided that a full and clear explanation of living conditions in England is given to each employee. This has been done and a very large number of men have accepted and arrangements for the necessary Travelling Permits are under way.'[33]

The weight of Irish labour during the war years must have been considerable as it is estimated that approximately 100,000 Irish migrants travelled to Britain during the years of the hostilities.[34] In this time the feats of the Ford entities in Britain make startling reading:

> Between the outbreak of hostilities in September 1939 and VE Day on 8 May 1945, Ford had built 137,483 tractors, which represented 95 per cent of all the wheeled tractors made

in the UK during the war. Ford had also produced 184,579 wheeled vehicles, 13,942 Bren-gun carriers and tracked vehicles, 250,000 V8 engines and 30,000 Merlin engines, among numerous other projects.[35]

Notably, the war production concerns operated in the shadows of the more dominant centre of Ford headquarters at Dagenham where in 1939 there were just 12,000 employed, but by spring 1945 there would be a head count of 34,163.[36] It is a pity to note that for a long time, because of sensitivities regarding Ireland's neutrality and Anglo-Irish relations generally, the important contribution of Irish migratory workers during World War II was largely ignored by both states. Thankfully, the record has been somewhat corrected in more recent times.

During the war years Ireland provided Britain with, what Enda Delaney has referred to as 'a reservoir of unskilled male and female labour'.[37] The Second World War was also important to Irish migrants as it changed the range of occupations open to the workers. Traditionally, Irish male workers had been engaged in heavy labour and their female counterparts took up positions in domestic service. John Jackson's survey of the Irish in Britain used the 1951 census to show the more diverse occupations held:

> Before the war the new arrival was almost bound to go into 'the building', general labouring or domestic service. Industrial occupations, transport, catering and the like were now open to the Irish worker. The war served the purpose of opening the way for far greater occupational choice and mobility for the Irish immigrant [*sic*] to Britain and paved the way for direct Irish infiltration into almost every branch of industry in the period since the end of the war.[38]

This can be seen as one way in which the 'Dagenham Yanks' diverge from the typical pattern of Irish migrants. The vehicle engineering industry, considered a 'new' industry, had established an importance in Cork pre-dating the Second World War by a decade.

It is clear too that the need for Irish labour continued in the post-war boom that Britain experienced. It was a time when expansion influenced industries from electricity supply to chemicals to construction. With specific regard to the motor industry it is interesting to note that in 'the absence of European competition and in a world lacking the dollars to purchase American vehicles, Britain became the world's leading exporter, selling abroad some 70 per cent of the 783,672 vehicles (522,515 cars and 261,157 commercial vehicles) produced in 1950.'[39] In the twelve-year period from 1945, the Ford Motor

Company invested over £100 million worth of capital equipment in Dagenham alone: in 1946 about 400,000 vehicles were produced there, by 1955 that figure had grown to 1,400,000.[40] Between 1948 and 1959 the output of the British car industry increased by 180 per cent: there was only an 18 per cent growth in the workforce.[41]

The 'Dagenham Yanks' form a part of Cork history that has been largely disregarded by commentators, even though they are an important part of the city's past. Dagenham became a safety net for many families affected by the lay-offs at the Marina plant, as well as those not working in the Cork factory when they failed to secure the all-too-scarce employment that existed in the area. Interestingly, some individuals, who would later become important players in Ford management in Britain and Europe, had started in their calling at the Leeside establishment. The careers of many men who started in Cork reiterate the pivotal role of migration in the history of Ford in Britain.[42]

In assessing the overall historical implications of the 'Dagenham Yanks' it is important to note certain points. The mass migration of individuals and families from the city of Cork would have occurred, no doubt, in the absence of the Ford, Marina and Dagenham connection. This was decreed by the economic constraints of the entire country during the decades in question. However, the route between Cork and Essex established itself much earlier in the Leeside city than in other areas and at that, long before the more pervasive impact of the global conflict of the Second World War. The paradigm, as exemplified by the 'Dagenham Yanks', was in no way unique to their home city. The traits and behaviour of the Irish migrant were universal, while obviously not totally homogenous. In this case, however, their special significance is in how the movement occurred largely under the aegis of the Ford entities of Ireland and Britain.

The migration to Dagenham, in particular, either sporadically or more long term, provided continuity of employment which would not have been possible on the Marina alone and it clearly had important implications for the standard of living and welfare of Cork Ford workers and their families. The fact that wage rate changes in Dagenham made their way into the columns of the main Cork newspaper is one very visible indication of the strong Cork-Dagenham link.[43] The Ford migrants are easily lost in statistics of mass departure that took place from Ireland to Britain during the twentieth century and so it is important to recall that their distinctiveness is not in terms of the actual figures involved as such, but rather in their major influence in the realms of employment, migration and remittances to the city of Cork over four decades. An extract of the lyrics from a ballad written by a 'Dagenham Yank', GusMcLaughlin, provide insightful reflections on life as a Ford migrant:

At seventeen years, I had no fears as I sailed from Penrose Quay,

Nor did I shirk, a strong man's work in the Dagenham factory,

There were men from every nation in the 20,000 force

You can take it from me, the foundry were all Irishmen, of course,

From the office door to the furnace floor, the accent, as a rule,

Was the one you'd meet down Patrick Street, Blackrock or sweet Blackpool.

There were tinkers, tailors, jewellers, bakers, I knew a solicitor too,

Didn't matter at all, whether furs or shawls were the clothes your mother knew,

At the fettlin' [fettling] wheel, you ground your steel with the smoke, the heat and the smell,

I saw strong men drop in the knockout shop. It was only one step from hell.

Half hour on, half hour off was how they worked the shift,

Till your eyes were red and your poor feet bled and your lungs near came adrift,

But Paddy from Cork could handle the work: with the heart he earned his pay.

'Twasn't much he spent for most of it went, across the Irish Sea.

Memories of the Marina

'They will never ... never leave me. They will always be with me: my days in Fords.'
Denis Forde, 2002 [1]

'I had often been bothered by the sense that, in fieldwork, I was somehow vampirizing my sources, sucking the voice, pouring it into my tape, storing it in my cellar, appropriating it in many different ways. But it had never occurred to me to think of interviewees as vampires themselves, speaking through me, nesting within my own voice.'
Alessandro Portelli, 1993 [2]

By the early 1960s the Marina had been well developed by Fords. The main assembly building, with its unusual saw-toothed roof detail, had been extended in 1929 with a machine shop and a press shop building being added. This stood near a three-storey storage building (also added in 1929) with a similar roof to the main assembly building.[3] The service garage and boiler plant buildings were also still in use. The transformer station building had, at this point, been changed into a general and stationery store and housed the printing department. But, the physical structure of the Marina plant that dominated both the skyline and images of the city quays for well over 60 years is in many ways easy to document and explain. It is far more difficult, however, to capture a sense of life under the famous black saw-toothed roof.

The narrative hereafter aims to go beyond the analysis of the firm purely as a system of production that offered 'its workers wages, some security and fringe benefits, in exchange for a period of time spent working in the factory'.[4] The social relationships that developed both inside and outside the factory walls will now be examined.[5] In interview, one man described the Cork organisation as a 'meritocracy'.[6] This chapter aims to capture how this possible meritocracy may have worked.

In interviews, the opening question to Ford employees was, when and under what circumstances did you come to work in Henry Ford & Son Limited? It transpired that well over half had a family or personal link that had aided him in securing a job there. This was a similar situation to Coventry (and indeed Indiana) car workers.[7] This practice seems to have had a long history in Cork although, in the period around the Second World War and earlier, there is evidence to suggest that two people from one family could not work in the plant as they:

> wanted to spread out the labour round the city so much. 'Twas very rarely you'd get two brothers working in the factory, but then later on, in the nineteen fifties and sixties, I

suppose, and seventies, they didn't mind then. They'd take on two of the one family, no problem. It depended on your ability then.[8]

Clearly, the earlier practice did not endure long term.

For many, the longevity of a family succession was an immense source of individual pride. When men provided the number of years they had with the company, they often included in the calculation the years accrued by older family members or they listed the number of generations in the connection with the company or the various managing directors under whom they had served.[9] This would go a long way in explaining the phenomenon whereby, to outsiders looking on, certain families could have been considered 'Ford families', often having numerous family or extended family members maintaining links with the company, some of which exist into the present day.

In Cork, one man revealed that:

> Timed service … meant a lot to people in Ford for many of them had great service, you know. I mean, there was people down there that I worked with who were coming to 30, 35 years' service with the company and they, went back a long way, you know.[10]

Interview after interview stressed how the procurement of a job at the plant was the ultimate in job security and remuneration. One interviewee articulated what he suspects his late parents would have thought of his joining Fords in 1971:

> they certainly would have looked on the big employers, the traditional employers in Cork, and getting a job in one of those was a sign of upward mobility … because they would have known the … relative affluence- in the working class world anyway- that came with a job in Fords.[11]

As one gentleman put it: 'to have a job in Fords you were elected [made]'.[12] Another recalled: 'You always had to know somebody … But in those days, if you got into Fords or Dunlops you were made for life, absolutely, you'd a job for life … they were the two companies in Cork to work for.'[13] One former garage mechanic used the term 'escape' to describe his entering into Fords.[14] These sentiments were offered by many of his vocational colleagues who perceived a post in the Ford plant as a much more attractive work environment than lying on the damp, dirty floor of one of the city's garages. In the 1960s this led to 'a difficulty for the garages in the city. They were losing so many skilled tradesmen to the Ford Motor

Company'.[15] In keeping with the broader trends in education of the years in question, few had any third-level educational qualifications on entering the firm even in the 'office jobs' or management positions. This is not to suggest that education and training were unimportant or undervalued in the company. Full support, encouragement and often assistance in these areas were provided as a Ford employee and, of course, this had broader implications – 'If you worked in Fords and you left, you did well. It was a great training ground'.[16] Essentially a job in Fords was safe, secure and well paid:

> I remember going to a course in Brussels, very early, 'twould [it would] have been probably around 1969 or 1970 … there were fifteen of us on the course … there were two Irish fellas and the rest were all Europeans. And on the Monday they put up a chart on the board and they said which of these are the highest priority in your life and they listed all wages, salaries, things, the whole lot, you know what I mean? … And one of the bullet points was 'security'. Security of job. And of course the two Irish fellas put down security of job as number one. The Europeans didn't consider it. 'Twas down the bottom of the list. But that's how important it was in those days, you know what I mean? If you had a good job you held on to it. 'Twas as simple as that.[17]

It appears that the stress was more on ability to carry out the job – regardless of position within the company hierarchy – rather than a necessity for qualifications. This outlook may owe its origins to the Ford Motor Company's own founder who was a famously practical man himself, and often held a disregard for academics. At the local level this is seen a little in the assertion: 'A lot of knowledgeable people said that I was stupid to join Ford, because … 'twas sort of too ruthless and they didn't have a great reputation of embracing, with open arms, graduates.'[18] The positive effect of this indifference towards formal educational requirements is demonstrated in the career of one former director shows: 'For a guy that came in, in 1955, sweeping the floor in the parts warehouse … I kind of grew with the company and grew through it and eventually ended up as a director.'[19]

> There was every kind of a fella throughout the system because if you take the years, there was little employment in Cork and there were very few opportunities. So, the idea of going to third-level education or going to university, I won't say 'twas non-existent but 'twasn't too far from it. So a lot of that calibre of person went in to Ford.[20]

A basic Ford ethos – that had dated to the company's foundation- was that any person could be trained to do any task of the operation of the plant – at all levels:

Moulders? Core makers? Smiths? Machinists? Not in numbers to notice. The foundry superintendent asserts that if an immigrant, who has never even seen the inside of a foundry before, cannot be made a first-class moulder of one piece only in three days, he can never be any use on the floor; and two days is held to be ample time to make a first-class core maker of a man who has never before seen a core-moulding bench in his life.[21]

When questioned on working conditions many of the older informants referred to the strictness in the plant in the early years.[22] One ex-serviceman commented: 'I worked in aircraft during the war so it was a change to go to Fords because it was 'like a reform school when I went there … It was a tough place to work.'[23] This severity in the early years was mentioned often in testimonies:

the conditions were very strict and difficult in Fords, at that time. I know … from my father, listening to my father and his friends.[24]

Another said of Fords in pre-Union days: 'You'd never know like, if you stepped out of line you were just gone out the door. Without any notice or anything. Oh, 'twas tough'.[25]

The slow down in production requirements in Cork prompted the movement of workers across the Irish Sea where, more times than not, they availed of work in one of Ford's British operations – more often than not, Dagenham. The system that developed in this way was often mentioned in interviews. The term 'lay-off' was attributed to these temporary redundancies and it seems that for the first 40 years of operations in Cork, lay-offs were a fact of life for many employed there as the:

assembly operation, 'twas up and down and people were being laid off and, and a lot, quiet a number of them, once they were laid off, they got on the *Innisfallen* and went over to Dagenham working and then came back and they continued like that, you see, into the '50s. 'Twould [It would be] be the late fifties...before they got any sort of continual thing, do you see.[26]

These styles of production and industrial relations had their roots firmly planted in American management methods of the day and would mirror the direction towards which Henry Ford & Son Limited looked in the period up until the 1960s; largely under the direction of John O'Neill. Only two days after starting on the Marina, one man experienced his first lay-off:

See, there was a ship carrying stuff for the plant, for assembly and it hit the rocks in the harbour ... there was no work available so I was laid off. And, that began a series of lay-offs like that continued nearly up to ... the '60s ... you know. In slack times we'd be laid off ... It was normal. It was accepted, at that time, like, that there was no work'.[27]

Ford vehicles being off-loaded onto the Cork quays, circa 1960.

For the modern observer, descriptions of work conditions and employee policies such as these are archaic. But it is vital to remember that at worst, Fords would have been considered no worse, and were arguably exceedingly more desirable, than contemporary employers in their policies towards employees. Remember, Ford workers were paid at substantially higher rates than almost all others in the entire region. Is it likely that one was compelled to contend with less than ideal working conditions when the financial rewards were as good as those in Fords? It is has been suggested that, in other Ford locations, that management 'was actually prepared to pay high wages to keep unions out of the plant'.[28] An account of Detroit's Highland Park Plant, as far back as 1914, alludes to this:

> These pay conditions make the workmen absolutely docile. New regulations, important or trivial, are made almost daily; workmen are studied individually and changed from place to place with no cause assigned, as the bosses see fit, and not one word of protest is ever spoken, because every man knows the door to the street stands open for any man who objects in any way, shape or manner to instant and unquestioning obedience to any directions whatever.'[29]

Men in Cork were only too aware of this reality in the same way. Likewise, it is highly probable that these high-pay rates were a major factor that held unionisation of the company at bay for as long as it did:

> Much of the labour of England is unionised, and men are held strictly to their crafts. We have no crafts in our industries, and although we are not opposed to unions, we have no dealings with them, because there is nothing that they can furnish to aid us in our management. We pay higher wages than any union could demand for its members generally, we have steady employment, and we are not interfered with.[30]

In the working environment of a factory in the twentieth century, it is no surprise that the words 'strike' and 'trade union' were part of the vocabulary of the recollections. Although, going back again to the relatively small size of the Marina plant and the more tight-knit working relationships that this would ensure, industrial conflict would be nowhere as fierce or dramatic as the famous debacles that occurred throughout British plants in the same decades.[31] Nevertheless, it would be inaccurate to infer by this that Cork escaped the effects of labour militancy entirely. Many perceived much of the industrial conflict in the plant as a symptom of boredom. One man explained:

> a lot of it was caused, was generated from the fact that people were slightly bored and there was a certain hum-drum … atmosphere to their everyday work, and so on, and it was a bit of diversion and possibly, a show of defiance too, in a way from the workforce. I always had the contention that boredom was a major factor in many of those strikes, because the strikes themselves were usually very petty strikes, and could have been handled, I would think, a lot of them could have been handled at a negotiating table with a little bit of dialogue.[32]

Continuing in a similar vein, there was a consensus that many of the 'walk-outs' that occurred in the factory, in latter years especially, involved the grievance of either one or a small number of employees and more often than not, their colleagues 'went out' primarily in an act of solidarity. On the Marina an almost ridiculous situation sometimes ensued where, for example, the 'chassis line' or the 'paint shop' all 'went out' but the majority of individuals had no idea as to why they had done so, unless they were directly involved. This would explain comments – from one shop-floor worker – like: 'I did go out. I did go out when they had a proper grievance.'[33]

In reviewing certain trade union records pertaining to Henry Ford & Son Limited it became clear that unofficial stoppages were a frequent and ongoing occurrence. Typically a chronology of incidents was recorded in a similar vein to the following details of a stoppage by the sanders in the paint department in early 1973:

> At approximately 2.00p.m. the Shop Representatives told the undersigned that the sanders told them that they had handled 29 rejects up to 1.00p.m., that they were overworked and that they would not handle any more rejects that day.
> They were told that the Company would continue production in the normal way.
> At approximately 3.45p.m. the sanders stopped work when a reject came along and it took the Shop Representatives half an hour to get them back to work so that they could take up their complaints.[34]

Certainly, most interviewees were reluctant to use the word 'strike' and preferred looser terminology such as 'walk-outs' or 'downing-tools' when engaging in conversation on this topic. Whether this reflects selective memory or a genuine discomfort in placing the relatively minor disturbances in the Cork plant in the same league as more formal and divisive action in the Ford community globally is worthy of consideration.[35] More likely is the fact that there was never an official dispute on the Marina: a point that was reiterated often by management in interviews. Shulman and Chamberlain's labour relations analysis is useful in placing the industrial disputes on the Marina in a broader context when they remark:

> In any industrial plant, whatever may be the form of the political or economic organisation in which it exists, problems are bound to arise ... They are not incidents peculiar to private enterprise. They are incidents of human organisation in any form of society ... But an industrial plant is not a debating society. Its object is production. When

a controversy arises, production cannot wait for exhaustion of the grievance procedure ... production must go on.[36]

Commenting on this issue with regard to Henry Ford & Son Limited, one man was keen to assert:

To me, you work for a company. You must understand that that company must make a profit. If it doesn't, if it doesn't show a profit, why carry on? Why exist?[37]

Essentially, trade unions became established in Cork only after they had done so in Britain almost a decade before. Manchester's Ford aero engine plant, established during the Second World War, was pivotal in the trade union movement and made Ford history:

Since it was technically a government establishment under Ford management, it had to abide by undertakings made between the government and trade unions at the beginning of the war.[38]

So in December 1941, Ford-Britain signed an agreement with the Amalgamated Engineering Union and recognised trade unions for the first time. In 1943 Dagenham followed suit in acknowledging unionisation.[39] Agreements with unions were first enshrined on the Marina in 1950 – evidently only with the Irish Transport and General Workers' Union.[40] And, although this would become the largest and most powerful union in Fords, certainly by 1965 there were at least ten other trade unions in operation on the Marina.[41] But, the membership of some unions may have been as little as one solitary member.[42] Recognition of unions in Cork came about as a result of a factory strike at the time but it seems there was no very marked change in working conditions in the wake of their arrival.[43] Yet, one interviewee remarked that:

you had a new, more liberal regime, you see. There, was …. not so much in that slackening … in the rules and things. But you wouldn't be fired now. In the old days, if you were three days on the trot late, you'd be fired ... those sorts of things, you know? You could get a pass out if you wanted to go to a funeral or a Christening or you could get a day off for a wedding or something like that, you know.[44]

It should be noted that the pay rates in Ford were always higher than those of other commercial concerns in the locality. This situation, combined with employment shortages in Ireland for protracted periods during the plant's existence, made Fords a competitive place to get into.[45]

From the trade union records, one surmises that grievances centred on the usual labour relations rivalries and idiosyncrasies rather than much more. The bigger question of how the nature of work on a line affects the individual would require further study but is worth acknowledging when discussing management, trade unions and power struggles between them. One former director went as far as to say that:

> Up to the time that the unions became established, the management or the factory management in Ford were horrendously arrogant … they did anything they wanted to do with the labour force. And the swing to the other side, when the unions got dominant – the existing management couldn't handle that. They conceded and conceded and conceded. They just couldn't handle what is now normal management-trade union relationships.[46]

As one might speculate, assembly line in the Ford plant was a pivotal and vital epicentre. One man referred to it as 'the hub' of the entire plant. But its significance within the remit of production was non-negotiable and paramount: 'There should never be a stop, d'you know what I mean? If something went wrong, the lines can't stop, they must keep going.'[47] Another man explained that 'the line was your master … the line itself, ah dictated your speed'.[48] He continued in saying:

> 'twas a macho place, not only because it was all men but because of the nature of the work. Especially when you were dealing with metal, you know, its hard and … so you would get 'toughish' kinds of clients all right. A great variety of people, of course, but some people who were genuinely tough.[49]

The command of the moving assembly line essentially meant that there was no room for diversion from the task at hand as the production method required consistency to operate economically. Henry Ford's tenacity for optimal production is shown, for example, by the chassis assembly line which divides the process among the assemblers so that each operation was performed in seven minutes and 36 seconds – producing 300 complete chassis on each line in eight hours, as follows:[50]

1. Three men fix four mud-guards [sic.]- two on each side.
2. Six men, on a moving line fix rear spring to chassis frame.

A Ford Cortina passing through the newly installed and state-of-the-art paint oven.

An Anglia and a Cortina in the spray booth.

3. Two of three men place and fix the rear axle, connecting the rear spring to the rear-axle spring shackles – the other man simultaneously places and fixes the front-axle assembly under the chassis frame.

4. One of two men completes the fixing of the front-axle, places the two combined lamp-brackets and front mud-guards, and places the nuts on. The other places and fixes the mud-guard and fixes the mud-guard bracket truss-rods.

5. Two men place the nuts on the truss-rods and fix on the controller-lever rock-shaft.

6. One man fixes the front spring, tightens nuts and puts in four split pins.

7. Two men complete the fixing of the combined front fender-irons and lamp brackets.

8. Place one gallon of gasoline in the tank on the gasoline tank bridge.

9. Two men attach gasoline tank and a feed-pipe for the tank.'[51]

The process continues for another 37 steps when the eventually complete car is driven off the line.

Corkmen working on the engine line.

Over half a century later, another writer described:

> On the assembly line each worker is termed an operator, he works at a particular station
> and work is allocated to him at that station. He is surrounded by stacks of components
> and maybe a man is sub-assembling these for him. His job is to attach his components to
> the body shells as they come to him. Obviously the faster the line runs, the less time he
> has on any particular body shell, and consequently the smaller the range of tasks that he
> is able to do. If the line is running, for example, at 30 cars an hour, he is allocated two
> minutes work on each car that passes him.[52]

One former Cork worker, however, made a significant observation with regard to the logistics of operations on the Marina. This plant, for a long time, assembled all the requirements for the Irish market and therefore a much wider variety of operations would be required on the assembly line in Cork than in the bigger Ford outfits:

> they could be doing up to a dozen different tasks … and because of the variation then in models … they weren't doing the same tasks to every vehicle that passed. If three Escorts passed, let's say … they were … putting in window winders, there would be one man doing it on one side and another on the other side…crossing the line was to be avoided you see, so you generally had people working on one side of the vehicle only. So a man putting in window winders, he would be doing that on Escort cars, when it came to a Transit or a truck … it would be a different operation because it would be a different design … so the bigger the variety of vehicles coming down, the more difficult the job for the operative. Except that some operatives might not have anything to do to a Transit for example … so when a Transit was passing them, they were able to work back the line then get on to whatever was their next car.[53]

A Ford Cortina on the chassis line.

D-series trucks and a Transit Van on the line.

As the decades had passed after 1914, the process of constructing a vehicle had very obviously evolved. By the 1970s, an assembly line for vehicles normally consisted of about 100 work stations: this assembly line was normally divided into four sections containing a body, paint, trim and mechanical line.[54] The main processes on the line were as follows:

The body is constructed and parts such as the floor, sides and the roof are placed in a jig and are spot-welded together.

The rigid body is moved on a conveyor, along the body-line, where doors and wings are added.

The augmented body goes through the paint plant where it is de-greased, treated with zinc phosphate (to prevent rust) and painted with enamel primer followed by enamel 'top coat' paint. It is then oven dried.

It is then placed on the trim line where parts such as glass, electrical wiring, instruments, etc. are added. Simultaneously, but separately, the engine, axles and drive shaft have been assembled on the mechanical line, onto which the body is lowered and bolted to it.

After the electrical connections have been made, the vehicle can be driven off the line for testing.[55]

Cortinas being buffed in the body shop.

Men working on the Marina's engine line.

An electrically-welded body shell being conveyed to the metal finishing conveyor line in October 1967.

Huw Beynon's comments on his Ford experiences provide a very realistic sense of what it was like to work the line in more recent times:

> In the last minute or so a man working on the high-line in one of the Ford Motor Company's assembly plants has fitted a petrol tank into the shell of a car and is starting to fit another. A man on the Engine Dress is fitting his second gear box into the engine … There are worse jobs. On the struts for example – installing the suspension units, a quarter of hundredweight at a time. Bending down all day. Men have had hemorrhages from working on the struts. So they share the job around. There's another bad job on the trim lines – installing the headlamps. Sat [*sic*] on a little trolley with wheels on. Your head underneath the wheel arches. Being pushed along the line … The man on the Engine Dress has fitted his second gearbox and is onto his third. In the next six hours or so, perhaps while you are reading this book, he will have a coffee break – coffee from a machine- and a dinner break – in the canteen. And he will have installed another 200 gearboxes. Forty an hour, 320 a shift.'[56]

Recalling his first impressions of the Marina's shop floor, one director remembered:

> The overriding impression was the noise and the intensity of activity. And, the general route from the offices to the front gate was literally through the factory. So you went down the main aisle of the factory and that went along the edge of the body shop … it just is an unimaginable place for people who actually haven't experienced it. To hear the noise of the arc-welding … body panels being slapped into bucks before they're welded together … but just the general splash of sparks, of flame and fire and noise … It's the overwhelming experience … or impression that anyone comes away from that area with … and the smell. The unique smell, because on your right, as you walk down, you have the paint shop and all the evaporative smells that issued from that … very distinctive. And then you had the smell of the body shop, that sort of waxy burning smell … you walked down past that then and you passed the 'cut and sew' where they made up the upholstery for seats with 50 tailors around their Singer sewing machines, or whatever they were inside there.[57]

Human nature dictates that invariably the memories that we carry with us the longest are those of the people we meet and interact with. Donnacha O Dulaing writes in his biographical work:

The Escort and Cortina line in the 1970s.

Memories remain, even if relationships have been severed by time and separation. Now and then I meet old colleagues, and stories and names from the past are remembered. Maybe I only remember the good old days but I never forgot the advice of Marcus, the barber of Fords, 'Remember one thing Boy, remember it well. When the boss smells gas, we all smell gas'.[58]

When it came to remembering the personalities and characters that the interviewees had shared so much of their working lives with, their recollections were as varied and as colourful as one might imagine. It was when this topic was broached that I found the description of Studs Terkel's experiences (of collecting oral history) fitted mine the most. He concluded that in:

recalling an epoch, some 30, 40, years ago, [some] experienced pain, in some instances; exhilaration, in others. Often it was a fusing of both. A hesitance, at first, was followed by a flow of memories: long-ago hurts and small triumphs. Honours and humiliations. There was laughter, too.'[59]

The final assembly line, where rigid quality control inspection was carried out, October 1967.

Some spoken to had not thought of their former colleagues or their work place in years. For others, the reminiscences were never far from their mind. As one older gentleman accessed the recesses of his mind for memories of people and situations long forgotten, he commented: 'You bring it all back to me, you know'.[60]

John O'Donoghue inspecting a Cortina engine bay on the final assembly line, October 1967.

There was an immense respect and reverence almost from the interviewees, which was held for the many men who were considered to have been exceptionally skilled mechanics and engineers. There was sense of regret implied, though often not directly articulated, that the century's huge technological developments in automation had relegated the skill requirement of earlier generations of workers at the Cork plant. In essence, the de-skilling of the role of the car worker had come about with the growth of the moving assembly line globally and had seen the car worker become essentially a track worker.[61] The working conditions within an assembly plant, hallmarked by the repetitive nature of the work and the pace as constantly dictated by the assembly line must have been borderline intolerable for many:

> People had fewer choices out there … A lot of people had intelligence. They had skills … we had people who through sentimental or family ties wanted to live back home here in Cork. They didn't want the emigrant trail … They traded maybe the foreign opportunities for a job at home. They traded personality or individual independence, for economic … well-being'.[62]

It may be a slightly harsh, but worthwhile, consideration that car workers on an assembly line, who drove to their place of work, would have 'already exercised their highest level of skill for that day'.[63] With this in mind, it would come as little surprise that beside the stresses and strains of production figures and units per hour, an entirely separate world of escape grew. This was fondly relayed in testimony after testimony, where the narratives re-lived were largely based on the stories, friendships, jokes, nicknames, loyalties and camaraderie found within the plant's workforce. One man summed up his viewpoint, exclaiming with enthusiasm that it was:

> a revelation, I mean it was definitely like, I'd say if I came back a … reincarnation, I'd possibly would like to spend another five years in the factory.[64]

If there was one observation, above all others, repeated in almost all conversations on working with Fords, it was that regarding the sheer diversity and expertise that was found under the roof of the plant. All were only too quick to point to the immense talent and acumen that was found right throughout the organisation, and especially on the factory floor:

> They weren't robots, by any means, you know, it was an intelligent workforce, very flexible. Tremendous skills, which weren't always needed, in the particular jobs they were doing. But people had come in from various crafts and trades. And that happened right from the foundation of the company, I would say … because the pay was better in Fords, than in any of the trades outside.[65]

Another man described:

> Ah, 'twas a marvellous place to work, there was some marvellous people and there were highly intelligent people in Fords. In this respect, and I'm not specifically talking about the management structure, there were 'hourly paid' people in Fords, they could turn their hands to anything.[66]

This man pointed out that:

> You had a body of men there from all sections of the community and if you wanted to know anything, there was always somebody in the factory who was an expert on it. Whatever it was. It could be history, it could be gardening, plumbing, building, any repairs in your work, any repairs in your car, there was always somebody to ask.[67]

Because of the Ford pay rates, the hiring of men qualified and skilled in areas outside the remit covered by a vehicle plant was always more probable than it would be for other employers:

One man, who started on the factory floor of Henry Ford & Son Limited in 1947, holds claim as one of eight medical students of his peer group who ended up working on the Marina – and not in the field of medicine![68]

The multitude of interests and activities in a plant that contained a workforce of around 1,000 individuals for almost seven decades is clear and there grew up around Ford's social activities that could cater to every interest. And, of course, the variety of backgrounds from which employees came, ranging from the graduates of the local secondary or technical school to the many ex-servicemen demobbed after the war, was influential in harnessing all the different talents, personalities and traits found under the roof of Fords. Just one of the numerous examples of this is in the career of one ex-serviceman who would go on to work for the company for 37 years having served as a commando landing on the Normandy beaches on D-day.[69] Another gentleman, who would go on to head the security and safety aspects of the factory, had served in the Palestinian police force between 1946 and 1948, prior to starting on the Marina in 1949.[70]

The pursuits undertaken during the lunch break alone and thus confined to the plant itself, give some indication of Ford's impact beyond those of the assembly of vehicles:

Within that 30 minutes then, there were a lot of activities, sort of … inclusive, as it were. You could, you had men who just walked around the plant, some played cards, other fellas played football. Then there was always entertainment of some sort or other. We had one or two, particularly one man who gave … many a stirring performance down in what we called, the 'trim line'. And he would sing. And then you had the choir who were practicing in the paints and Sundays as well under their dedicated conductor ... People who said the Rosary as well and … and if you wanted to place a bet.[71]

As Paul Thompson points out, factory 'sociability was more than an escape from work: it was also an attempt to make the work world more fully human'.[72] One of my informants offered a comparable judgment in succinctly stating: 'if you didn't have a little bit of hilarity in the middle of it you'd have cracked up completely'.[73]

An element of class distinction was apparent and to be expected in a plant of its nature. Despite there being a certain demarcation between 'hourly paid' workers and those in receipt of a salary – which broadly mirrored those who worked on the factory floor and those with 'office jobs' – a mutual respect was evident. This may have gone back to the awareness that the continuity of the assembly line was imperative in maintaining production. This symbiotic relationship grew from the knowledge that the man on the 'trim line', for example, was as important as the sales man travelling the by-roads of Donegal. The medical student already mentioned, who had abandoned his studies to work in Fords and started off on the factory floor before moving into the offices, expressed that there was:

> a sort of … a class distinction. I mean there was one friend of mine who wouldn't look at me while I was out in the factory. This sort of envied pride, they were somebody even though some of the lads in the factory were making more than the lad in the office.[74]

A newly-qualified mechanic saw his move into the white-collar world from a slightly different perspective. When asked if he regretted leaving his mechanics job he was quick to say:

> Oh God no. At that stage, I had my knuckles dirty for six years, right … whilst it was very enthusiastic when you're fifteen or sixteen, with a view to go serving your time and to learn all about motor cars, right. It was now much more attractive to get into a suit, right.[75]

This more attractive work environment was coupled with a degree of upward mobility, so often evident in the progression into executive positions.

Undoubtedly, the passing of time softens even the harshest of critics of any organisation. But even with this in mind, the level of loyalty, admiration and respect when perceptions of Fords were elicited was astonishing. If the legacy of a company can be in any way judged by the attitudes of its former employees, Henry Ford & Son Limited can, even still, boast a generation of workers who was overwhelmingly positive with regard to their working years. Criticism leveled at the firm was negligible and hinged greatly around personality clashes rather than any more serious grievances.

Was there a conspiracy? Was there a level of self-selectivity detectable that was affecting the sample of interviewees? As the corpus of interviews grew and more diverse methods of contacting informants were used more hard-hitting questions were asked. The simple fact was that the criticisms expressed were so tremendously engulfed in the language of respect, affection and loyalty towards a firm and people many had shared 40 years with. It was a difficult task to extract any censure.

Those who did recall unpleasant experiences, bad days and bitter conflicts in the same breath rationalised these as natural and expected occurrences in the day-to-day of work and social interaction. And so, this situation led on to deliberation of matters related to connections between memory and cognition; truth, falsehoods and forgetfulness; and social and personal identity. Samuel Schrager's observations on storytelling in an Idaho community eased my discomfort in this regard somewhat:

> What we are telling seldom can be verified in a strict sense, even when we can produce supporting evidence. Ultimately, its validity rests less in its context than in social relationships. We agree to regard each other – at least some others – as bearers of truth. We accept what we are hearing even though it is not and never can be a literal transcription of events. Our expectation is that it will be faithful to the teller's knowledge, interpretation, and imagination, a realisation of his or her perceptions of what is significant and worth repeating to us at the time.[76]

The warmth with which informants spoke of their working lives, relationships and experiences with Fords was blatant and was found, not only within the confines of the formal interviews but also in the copious casual conversations that were had with others who had served in the Leeside site.[77] A lady who spent her entire working career with the company delighted in pointing out that:

Oh yeah, I'd never let anyone say a bad word about them [Fords] ... Even though, like, we fought our way and fought for things and that, but generally speaking, I couldn't speak highly enough of them.[78]

Another man concluded:

And as I say, the real test is that I'd do it all again ... ah yeah. Why not? 'Twas good for me and 'twas good for my family and 'twas good for Cork. Very good for Cork ... They were great employers, absolutely ... 'Twas a terrible wrench to leave the Marina, as I say, because, that was home.[79]

The notion of the Marina as a kind of 'home' was given more substance when the paternalistic attributes of the firm were so frequently alluded to. Examples of the firm's benevolence are scattered throughout the testimonies and range from the standard charitable contributions of an entity of its type in any locality to repeated individual instances of compassion and generosity far beyond the obligation of any employer in similar circumstances. A dramatic example of this is seen in the career of one informant who was hired by the company at the age of fifteen, to provide for the family, after his father had been accidentally killed while working in Ford's Leamington Spa foundry during the Second World War. Here he describes the company's management who had taken him on in 1943: 'I thought that they were the most compassionate, concerned, attentive management committee that Fords ever had.'[80] This man remained with the company into four decades with his son continuing the family tradition in latter years. Another teenager, employed under similarly tragic circumstances in 1938, moved up through the management ranks to eventually become a director of the company prior to his retirement in the 1980s.

There can be no doubt in any Cork person's mind that for the 67 years that the firm worked out of the Marina, its reputation as an employer was highly regarded: an attitude that was sometimes as much a result of the city's limited employment opportunities, at various times, as of the pay and employment conditions there. The Marina development marked an early, national example of what would later become a common phenomenon in Irish business and manufacture: the industrial estate.[81] Fords brought with them the most modern, American production methods and offered for the most part, and in latter years more particularly, secure, reliable employment in a favourable work environment, by the standards of the day. It is abundantly clear that the influence of Fords must have extended beyond the confines of the plant itself and was felt by other employers and thus workers in the city – as well as its impact in the realms of training and technical education.

The entrance to the Cork plant as it was in the late 1970s.

The physical traces of the plant are eroded more and more as the years pass and for this reason it is important to document something of what remains of this hugely imposing part of the city's twentieth-century history. One man referred to it as 'a tremendous slice of Cork life'.[82] Another is quoted as saying: 'it's silly to say it's a state of mind … it represents a tradition in the country, it represents a "Corkishness".'[83] In conclusion, Paul Thompson's reflections offer insights into the role of history and oral sources that are worth considering here:

> While historians study the actors of history from a distance, their characterizations of their lives, views and actions will always risk being misdescriptions [*sic*.], projections of the historian's own experience and imagination: a scholarly form of fiction. Oral evidence, by transforming the 'objects' of study into 'subjects', makes for a history which is not just richer, more vivid, and heart-rendering, but *truer*.[84]

One thing that is clear is that the memories were 'both private and official, symbolic and real, literal and layered. They were as complex as the past they represented'.[85]

The Cork Plant's Final Epoch

'Not a single item of equipment can be regarded as permanent.
Not even the site can be taken as fixed.'
Henry Ford, 1930[1]

'Once we joined the EEC, the clock started ticking as far as Ford was concerned, and from then on it was only a question of which month, which day and whether it would be 1984 or 1985.'
The Irish Times, 1984[2]

The decision behind the location of Henry Ford & Son Limited in Ireland was one that largely hinged on the favourable economic conditions as they existed at the time. More explicitly, this condition was that Ireland 'was next door to, and had free access to, the world's most affluent market'.[3] This economic status was disrupted with the formation of the Irish Free State in the severing of political links with Britain, along with the ensuing tariffs, as they were applied to the manufacture of vehicles. One historian outlines the progress by 1927 in stating:

> Cumann na Gaedheal's economic policy was committed towards continuing the post-famine pattern of close trading connections with Britain with consequent emphasis on agriculture and food based export industries – a beer, biscuits, cars and cattle coalition – and a continuing sterling link. Tariff protection had been depoliticised and was no longer on the agenda.[4]

To recapitulate, the 1920s had begun as a turbulent decade on the Marina. The Ford Cork operation had been established during the latter part of a major global conflict. It subsequently survived the War of Independence, a civil war and a serious clash with local power-holders. Tractors had come and gone and now they had come back again. By mid-1932 though, the future was less certain. Just over two years earlier the plant employed about 7,000 workers who were busily involved in the manufacture of vehicles ranging from cars to trucks and tractors, as well as parts. By the summer months of 1932 among other things, the company was under the direction of a new manager in John O'Neill; the workforce had been decreased seven-fold and the foundry was redundant after the tractor works were removed again. Cork would now revert to its former role in assembly for the domestic market. Observers must have viewed cautiously what lay ahead for the Marina, especially in light of the opening of the huge Dagenham facility on the neighbouring island. Moreover, the combined effects of the Great Depression, the Economic War between the Irish Free State and Britain and the protectionist policies pursued by government, had a major impact on Henry Ford & Son Limited.

The newly elected government embarked on an 'Economic War' with Britain – which reduced trade between the two countries at a time when trade was already hit by the worldwide economic depression. This also contributed to the switch from a long established position of free trade to an experiment in protectionism and economic nationalism. A spiral of events started in May 1932 with the Finance Act 'imposing *ad valorem* duties ranging from 15 to 75 per cent on 38 classes of goods, with specific duties on other classes'.[5] If the Economic War is seen as an essentially political campaign, it also had huge economic implications.[6] The tariffs introduced in the budget of 1932, which imposed a high duty on the import of motor vehicles and tractors, were quickly countered by retaliatory measures by the British government. This move was followed by the home government's enforcement of 'emergency duties' applied exclusively to British imports. At a local level, the components being imported into Cork from Dagenham now carried a 70 per cent duty, adding £40 to the price of some cars.[7] The reaction of Sir Percival Perry (by now, director of Ford operations in Britain and Ireland) showed how the company viewed the new status:

> The business of Henry Ford & Son Limited at Cork, Ireland, is principally export, and our hopes and aspirations have been to build up a large Empire and foreign trade in Fordson tractors manufactured in the Irish Free State. When deciding upon this enterprise we envisaged a clear economic atmosphere. Taking the long view, we are not pessimistic as to the future world demand for our product; but recent events may react upon our plans, policies and prospects, and we regard the changed political outlook in the Free State with grave concern and apprehension.[8]

All indications would be that the withdrawal of the tractor business from Cork was linked to the changed political and economic status of the island. Henry Ford actually alluded to this himself in one of his works: 'it was designed to manufacture tractors for distribution through Europe, but free production was so hampered by politics that we changed the whole plant.'[9] The use of the Dagenham plant could not be surprising in such an environment. In a similar move, Guinness' transferred beer production to the Park Lane brewery near London in the 1930s after the erection of tariffs. Here, the British tariffs 'led to the establishment of an efficient new factory in England, at the expense of Ireland'.[10]

For obvious reasons, both imports and exports of manufactured goods dropped after 1932. It has been concluded that the impact of import substitution on trade was lessened by the reliance on imported parts

9 September 1936 – Official visit by Eamon de Valera, accompanied by Frank Aiken (Minister for Defence), Hugo Flinn, T.P. Dowdall TD, George Crosbie (Directors of the Cork Examiner*). On Mr de Valera's left is John O'Neill, Managing Director, Henry Ford & Son Limited. The president was in Cork to open the new City Hall, rebuilt after its destruction in December 1920.*

and raw materials. This had come about under the 1934 Control of Imports Act that imposed quota restrictions preventing the importation of f.b.u. (fully-built-up) vehicles. It was with these quota restrictions and duties that the motor vehicle assembly sector could continue unhindered for over 30 years in Ireland. Fords had become, like most of the other firms in the country at the time, an assembly unit for foreign-produced parts. In fact, one economic historian draws specifically on the motor business as an example of this dependence on imported parts:

> This was particularly so in vehicle assembly, where the trade in 'motor vehicle chassis imported as parts' and 'motor vehicle bodies imported as parts' loomed large. These were

also known as 'CKDs' (for 'completely knocked down vehicles).[11]

This would go a long way to explain the situation where the 'aggregate value of finished manufactured imports fell by one-seventh, while the value of raw materials and semi-prepared goods imported rose by one-fifth in the period between 1932 and 1938'.[12] In spite of the surrounding constraints Ford production and sales figures steadily, if gradually, grew from August 1932 onwards.[13] The new Model Y was launched in the following spring.

The city of Cork saw the City Hall reopened by President de Valera on Tuesday 8 September 1936, over sixteen years after the previous building had fallen victim to the city's burning by British forces. The head of state availed of his official visit to the city to make a detailed tour of inspection of Henry Ford & Son Limited. Here, the party was shown the latest models as well as being introduced to the company's newly-implemented purchasing plan. This policy saw Fords manufacture and purchase at a local level as far as was possible in each country of operation. The *Cork Examiner* described the visit as follows:

> The President listened attentively as Mr O' Neill explained that to inaugurate this scheme in Ireland Messrs. Henry Ford and Son, Ltd., Cork, invited Irish manufacturers to submit samples and quotations for the supply of a wide range of parts and materials required in the production of Ford cars and trucks at the Cork works.[14]

By 1937, sales of Ford vehicles in Ireland had increased to record levels. Private car registrations for that year saw the brand secure 5,893 sales.[15] The nearest rivals in Morris and Austin had only sold 1,352 and 811 cars respectively in the same period.[16] 1938 would be a good year for the company. On 17 January the plant would build her 25,000[th] car.[17] In celebration of Henry Ford & Son Limited's twenty-first birthday an 'Open House' began on 19 April with members of the public being encouraged to visit the plant.[18] This milestone marked the period in which over 73,000 vehicles had been produced in Cork since 1919 and 'a million pounds spent in the purchase of Irish materials, while the colossal sum of £6,000,000 has been paid out in wages and salaries.'[19] Newspaper reportage of de Valera's visit, the 25,000[th] vehicle and the plant's twenty-first birthday, provide very interesting insights into the company's outlook and how it wanted to be perceived as a commercial entity. The stress that was constantly placed on the factory's use of local labour, products and services is glaring. Every opportunity was availed of to highlight this.[20] And when this is viewed in the context of the keenly nationalist industrial policy of the government, it is easy to understand why Fords was keen to stress the company's 'Irishness' and integration into the local economy.

The 25,000th Ford built at Henry Ford & Son Limited, on 17 January 1938. Seen with the car are, on the left, John O'Neill, Managing Director, and R.W. Archer, Ireland's first Ford dealer (in the bowler hat).

The Economic War concluded with the Defence, Financial and Trade Agreements signed on 25 April 1938. By this time, Ford Cork's production of vehicles had gone from the 1932 figure of 498 to 7,454 for 1938.[21] But just as trade relations with Britain normalised, the outbreak of the Second World War produced the next serious disruption of the world economy. This would affect economic policy and performance for almost a decade and drastically reduce production on the Marina. Irish neutrality would ensure that the country would remain relatively untroubled by the crisis that the September 1939 declaration led to. But submarine warfare would soon threaten supplies and shipping was naturally restricted. All industry was severely hit by fuel and machinery shortages and the scarcity of materials. In total, material shortages meant that industrial production fell in Ireland by almost 30 per cent and industrial employment by 15 per cent during the years of conflict.[22] For business such as that at Fords, where there was a heavy dependence on the import of semi-finished goods for assembly, it would simply mean that production would have to cease. And it did. The shortages of raw materials, energy and spare parts during the war had a major impact on sectors such as vehicle assembly, engineering and chemicals in Ireland: 'Near-autarky was worse than protection.'[23]

By mid-1941, Ford production and sales had fallen to less than a quarter of those for the same period in 1940, and service parts for existing vehicles were becoming increasingly difficult to obtain.[24] An outcome of this shortage of supplies saw Fords recycle steel from old tramways and make screwdrivers out of old valve stems.[25] The engine and parts reconditioning department became an important venture in the plant: one worker who was hired during the period referred to it as the 'mainstay of the factory throughout the war years'.[26] The land on the factory estate on the Marina was used to produce the vegetables, corn and beet that were grown and sold at local markets and also supplied the plant's canteen.[27] Other activities, as diverse as nail-straightening and saving and selling turf were also undertaken:

> We have placed 150 and are hiring a further 30 of our unemployed workers on turf production to protect our own company's fuel supplies and also the domestic requirements of our workers. The surplus, if any, would of course be made available to the public. An experiment will be made by the Midleton (County Cork) Gas Company for us in producing peat charcoal for sale to users of producer gas outfits on trucks, the Gas Company taking the peat gas for mixing with their town supply. We are endeavouring to secure a forest to enable us to transfer these men during the winter period and others will be used to repaint the interior and exterior of our factory if sufficient paint can be obtained. [28]

Fuel rations progressed to the elimination of private motoring with only doctors and clergymen being exempt from the prohibition of the use of cars. This would see the number of new private cars licensed for use drop from 7,480 in 1939 to 240 in 1941.[29] For the Ford operation, production of 3,358 vehicles in 1940 dropped to 863 vehicles the following year and only 176 in the first half of 1942.[30] Despite all best efforts, production ceased on the Marina from June 1942 and it would be almost four years before it would resume again. By this time there was a minimal staff level maintained. Employee records of white-collar workers note a mass exodus from Cork to work for Ford in Britain, especially from 1941 onwards.[31] Presumably, this level would have been the last to be discharged and the plant workers and lower level white-collar workers would have been made redundant prior. The impact of the Second World War on the sphere of migration from Cork, and more specifically from Henry Ford & Son Limited to Dagenham, has been largely covered. It is clear that the majority of Ford employees who were put out of work in Cork during the conflict, made the journey to Dagenham, Leamington Spa or Manchester simply to maintain continuity of employment.

Another conflict left its mark on the Marina. And so, yet again, in early 1946, it was time for the company to regroup and look to its future. It seems that the plant was relatively prompt in re-establishing itself, despite its miniscule workforce and its break in production. The *Cork Examiner* happily carried the announcement of the first post-war vehicle as it came off the assembly line in February that year:

> This was the first output of the works since the world war interrupted their vast productive capacity and limited them to the servicing of vehicles then on the road. For this latter purpose only a skeleton staff was maintained throughout the war years.[32]

The motor business gradually got back on its feet and the number of cars registered rose from 2,848 in 1946 to 17,524 in 1950'.[33] By the end of the 1949 season, Cork announced that for the first time in the company's history more than 10,000 vehicles had been sold on the domestic market.[34]

The second half of the century began in Cork with an optimistic start at Henry Ford & Son Limited. At 2.15pm on 18 July 1950, the longest-serving employee, Bill O'Connell, drove the 75,000[th] vehicle built in Cork since 1932 off the assembly line.[35] This event was witnessed by 150 long-service employees who could boast a combined service of 4,000 years of continuous employment with Henry Ford & Son Limited: an impressive feat by any standards.[36] Since its opening on the Marina in 1917 the company had by this time contributed £8 million to the Cork economy in wages and salaries and had made purchases in the region of £3 million in the process of manufacturing over 123,000 vehicles.[37] On the production front, the war was becoming a distant memory as production figures and sales continuously grew in the immediate post-war years. Unconvincing production figures of 2,379 in 1946 paled beside those of 11,007 and 11,881 in 1949 and 1950 respectively.[38] Yet, this optimism was a little unstable:

> Much of the consumer boom was fuelled, not by increases, but by the enforced savings of the war years. The amount of money in bank deposits had risen during the war and this was now spent when consumer goods such as cars, again became available.[39]

In the meantime, it was a positive time for Fords. The variety of vehicles assembled in Cork ranged from the low-priced and economical Anglia car to the luxury V8 custom saloon to several vans, Thames trucks and, of course in Ireland, tractors. From a practical point of view and as mentioned in the previous chapter, an assembly line that would cater for this diversity of vehicles and their derivatives must have been – and was recalled so in interviews– as an extremely complex and well-organised accomplishment.[40]

Economic historians and commentators have been critical of the manner by which Irish industries, at this time failed to venture beyond the domestic market. As has been pointed out:

> The only escape from this dependence on the stagnant home market lay in expanding exports. By the 1950s, however, most firms were accustomed to tariff protection and had become complacent and comparatively inefficient.[41]

With this charge Henry Ford & Son Limited could escape criticism. From at least 1955 onwards there were vehicles being exported from Cork to Northern Ireland, the United States and Finland.[42] These exports – while not huge in numbers – were not only of passenger cars, but trucks and ambulances also. Remember too that Cork had a proven track record in the realm of tractor export that dated back to 1919 or 1920.[43]

The fiftieth anniversary of the Ford Motor Company was celebrated in Cork in June 1953 with an 'Open House' on the Marina.[44] But the following year was probably more exciting locally. The head of the Ford empire, Henry Ford II, paid a visit to Cork. Arriving in Shannon Airport on 30 August, he was accompanied by dignitaries from Ford of Britain. Over 40 years before, Henry II's father and grandfather had holidayed in the city in a quiet and private way, with no fuss or fanfare. This was not the case for this Ford visit. Press and photographers waited at the airport to welcome the party before they were whisked off to their destination. On arrival in the city the magnate was greeted by striking protestors. Management had in recent days closed Henry Ford & Son Limited after 400 workers had ceased work demanding a wage increase.[45] Despite pressure placed by the workers to involve the company's chief in negotiations and perhaps to use his visit as leverage in the politics of the dispute, local management remained resolute. In the end the row was resolved within days, and production resumed, but the entire event undoubtedly overshadowed what should have been a much happier occasion. The pay demands of workers who started on a basic weekly wage of over £6 must have been viewed with a degree of scepticism by onlookers, most especially in a climate where securing any even modestly paid employment was difficult.[46] An editorial in the *Cork Examiner* expresses a particularly middle class view of the visit:

> But that Mr. Ford, who personifies an organisation which has contributed more than any other single factor to the prosperity of Cork and the high standards of living enjoyed by Cork workers should have entered our city under a cloud, is, to say the least of it, deplorable.[47]

The entire episode gathered a folkloric entity in the world of Henry Ford & Son Limited. It featured as a frequent story recalled in the oral interviews undertaken. The slogan 'Workers starve while bosses feast' – that had donned the banners of the strikers outside the Imperial Hotel as Henry II arrived – took on a mantra-like status in recollections. And related to this was the reminiscence regarding the protestor's spokesperson: Michael Cremin. The title of his position in Fords is enshrined in the lore of the Cork plant and was passed down through generations of employees. It was surprising to see this also printed in the *Cork Examiner*:

> Their spokesman, Mr Michael Cremin said that a man coming in on the production line was paid the basic wage of £6/6/10 (less 2/4 insurance). Describing himself as 'an automobile optician' – because he put the glass in cars – he said that he was a married man with two children and that his weekly wage was £9/0/6. He has been employed in the firm for 25 years.[48]

With the stroke of a pen, the 'automobile optician' assured his place in Ford history.

The sixth decade of the twentieth century has been viewed as one where 'brief outbursts of optimism (as in early 1955, for example) were replaced by long bouts of gloom'.[49] It was overall an equally mixed bag in the Cork factory. They had managed to restart after the major interruption of the Second World War. Ford had carved for itself a role as an Irish market leader by securing, almost invariably, around one-third of the car market and an even higher proportion in commercial vehicles, going back as far as 1946.[50] Now they were dabbling in the export trade. But the system of production in Cork meant that the frequent lay-offs and the ensuing migration – that had become a hallmark of life in 1950s' Ireland – left a huge mark on the Marina. It seems that at this time the plant, still under John O'Neill, followed American trends in production and employment. Essentially, the hiring and firing of workers followed the pattern set by the cycle of the motor industry with its ups and downs. As demand increased, usually in the summer months, people were taken on. Towards the latter end of the year, business would slow and the workers who were surplus to requirement were 'laid-off'.[51] It was this system that principally made England such a vital lifeline to so many Cork families.

In essence, the lay-offs were induced by fluctuating commercial demands under the broader economic conditions. An example of this can be seen with the Suez Crisis in the mid-1950s. The events surrounding General Nassar and Egypt took on a new relevance in Cork during this tense time when it lead to short-time working hours and redundancies, affecting both plant and office staff.[52] Employment figures on the Marina went from 745 on 1 January 1956 to 559 on 22 June of the same year.[53] John O'Neill outlined other measures that were also taken at the time:

> In an endeavour to retain employees his firm had engaged in the building of vehicles for stock and they now had some 700 vehicles on hand. This represented about two months' supply as against their normal holding of three weeks'. In addition, employees were being held on and put to work on various types of unproductive labour.[54]

The export figures for the same period show that there were only 61 vehicles exported from Cork in 1956 whilst there had been 1,199 the previous year.

This also highlights the role of external issues on the dynamics of economics on the wider national and international levels. Louis Cullen's economic history has this issue in mind: 'The economy was particularly vulnerable to external political events, and the fiscal crises of 1951-3 and 1956-7 correspond to the superimposition of the effects of the Korean War in 1950-1 and of the Suez crises of 1956-7 on broader, adverse economic developments.'[55] Nonetheless, Henry Ford & Son Limited had survived another test. 1959 saw Seán Lemass succeed de Valera as Taoiseach and a Cork man, a 'Dagenham Yank' of sorts, Tom Brennan, was in charge on the Marina.[56] In more ways than one, a new era began.

In June 1961, the CIO (Committee on Industrial Organisation) was set up, drawing membership from industry, trade unions and the public service. Its purpose was 'co-ordinating arrangements for a comprehensive survey of the industrial sector, directed towards an examination of the difficulties which might be created for particular industries should this country enter the Common Market, and the formulation of positive measures of adjustment and adaptation'.[57] Within the framework of this organisation, working teams were appointed to survey various industries with the motor assembly sector as one selected for study. At this time there were 22 assemblers in the country. In Fords, an internal group was convened to make similar assessments in relation to their own particular commercial interests.[58]

The results of the CIO report were less than encouraging which is hardly surprising in light of the protected nature of the sector since its inception. A draft copy of the report sheds an informative light on the circumstances:

> We accept the conclusions of the Survey Team that the motor vehicle assembly industry would have no economic prospects of survival under free trade conditions and that the

commercial vehicle body building industry would be badly hit. The principal question at issue, therefore, is whether effective action can be taken in the interval by the existing employment for the workers likely to be disemployed [*sic.*].[59]

Following the publication of the report, meetings were held with representatives from the industry, where they were reminded of their 'responsibilities to their workers and that they were under an obligation to consider all possible measures to prevent the occurrence of serious unemployment on cessation of the assembly industry'.[60] It was clear that Fords took this consideration seriously and that alternative roles for the Marina would be considered before 1984.[61] Trade liberalization began in 1963 and 1964 when tariffs were reduced.[62] As a consequence of the Anglo-Irish Free Trade Agreement in 1965, Ireland agreed to phase out tariffs on British industrial goods over a ten-year period. However, motor assembly was exempt from this restriction. Regarding motor assembly, a combined effort on the part of the Irish government, unions, the assembly companies, British manufacturers and the British Board of Trade bore fruit in a special scheme controlling importation of fully built up vehicles (f.b.u.). The basic tenet of this plan 'was the channelling of imports of fully built up (f.b.u.) vehicles at substantially reduced rates of duty, through registered importers/assemblers who undertook to maintain a volume of assembly equivalent to the 1965 level'.[63] A temporary reprieve had been brokered.

The entrance lodge and the car despatch area of Henry Ford & Son Limited in October 1967.
It was here that vehicles awaited distribution to Ford dealerships throughout the country.

Meanwhile, on the Marina, production and sales were on the up. In 1966, 11,041 out of 39,546 new car owners had bought a Ford from one of the 82 dealerships across the country. Production had averaged at approximately 10,000 vehicles annually in the decade ending in 1958.[64] The same interval following would see this figure average at 13,500 per annum.[65] Overall, increased demand saw production increase by over 200 per cent in the years between 1956 and 1966.[66] Fords experience of this boom in cars sales was part of a general increase in demand for cars.

The Ford Cork plant now assembled fourteen passenger models and various commercial vehicles also. Concurrently, on foot of the various studies undertaken in the national sphere, specific recommendations were made on the steps needed to prepare industry for foreign competition.[67] The awareness of the impact that the changing markets would have on Fords was clear and the company must have been only too delighted to avail of government initiatives in modernising. In this, in the region of £2 million were spent and made Henry Ford & Son Limited the largest and most modern assembly plant in the country.[68] Taoiseach Jack Lynch's comments opening the newly-upgraded facility and marking the fiftieth anniversary of Henry Ford & Son Limited reflect a political consensus of the era:

> With the inevitable approach of free trade and the prospect of membership of the European Economic Community, other sectors of Irish industry will have to take similar action appropriate to their circumstance if they are to hold their share of the home market and at the same time achieve the expansion of exports on which our economic prosperity depends.[69]

These years marked a new optimism, reflected in a more visible sense of community springing up on the Marina. This new outlook culminated in many initiatives where buzz words such as 'teamwork' and 'spirit' would become common language; where the organisation of a 'Ford Sports Day' became an important annual event; and a suggestion scheme was implemented for workers and sporting trips between Cork and Dagenham were arranged. Another topical development was the plant's 1967-launched monthly in-house newspaper – *Ford News*. This publication reflects many of the social spheres that the company and Ford workers touched. An eclectic variety of pursuits and interests lined its pages and it was seen as a means by which the hitherto fragmented nature of these activities could be gathered together on one platform. In its first issue, Tom Brennan outlined the goals of the organ in stating:

> That it would improve the family spirit throughout the whole organisation so that people would realise they are part of a team and that the whole future of the organisation depends on the skills and loyalties of the team members, one to another.[70]

Jack Lynch watches operations on the line during his visit in October 1967.

All these changes marked pro-active schemes that would reassert the fact that the Ford factory in Cork was much more than a place of work for its 1,000-plus employees and that its sphere of influence stretched into the families and lives of the city in a much more extensive manner beyond the pounds and pence of weekly wages. Probably the most striking feature of the *Ford News*, right from its inception to the final editions in 1984, were the columns devoted to long-service awards and obituaries. These, more than any other source, are a remarkable testament to the generations of men and women who had invariably worked on the Marina over two, three and sometimes four decades. Notices, such as the one following, were not at all unusual and demonstrate the credentials of a typical 'Ford Family':

> Deep regret has been occasioned by the death, after a prolonged illness, of Mr. Patrick Twomey, 4 Cathedral Walk, Cork, who was employed by the company for 35 years, most of which time he spent in the Paint Department. He is survived by his widow, and also

by a son, Mr Patrick J. Twomey, a member of the Restaurant Staff. He was brother of Mr. William Twomey, a Ford employee at Dagenham, and uncle of Mr Patrick Twomey, one of our maintenance painters.[71]

Notices such as this show how a long service 'meant a lot to people in Ford for many of them had great service, you know? I mean there was people down there – that I worked with – who were coming up to 30, 35 years service with the company and they went back a long way, you know'.[72]

Sir Patrick Hennessy (far right), Jack Lynch, Paddy Hayes (centre), Lord Mayor P. Wyse and Bishop Simms (in background) are shown around the newly-extended Henry Ford & Son Limited plant in October 1967.

To return to economic matters, it is natural to assume that the developments in Europe would have impact beyond Ford's operation in Ireland. A writer on Ford in Europe explains:

It was also noticeable to Ford executives that the organisation in the 1960s, with sales companies in fourteen European countries and major manufacturing centres in Britain and Germany, had limitations. The evolution of the company's activities in Europe so far had had to accord with national boundaries and the practicalities of a continent divided by frontiers. The changing economic shape in Europe called for a new approach. With this in mind, in June 1967, a new company, *Ford of Europe*, was created. Its task was to co-ordinate all Ford's European activities and would allow the organisation run 'on a functional rather than a geographic basis.[73]

In light of the economic outlook and policies pursued in Ireland in the preceding years, the absorption of Henry Ford & Son Limited into this new company (the umbrella-like structure of Ford of Europe) dovetailed nicely.

Jack Broderick of Ballyphehane receiving a retirement presentation from his Body Assembly colleagues in April 1974, after 43 years service. Dan Spillane (centre left) is making the presentation, with Tim O'Callaghan (centre right).

Tom Brennan handed over the reins to Paddy Hayes in 1971.[74] As EEC membership loomed in the not-too-distant future, it was clear that existing methods of assembly needed to be changed. Up to this point, Cork still assembled the entire range of cars and trucks, despite the fact that the plant may only have produced three or four vehicles of certain models in a day. Obviously, the economics behind such a method were far from desirable in an industry where economies of scale in production are highly significant.[75] Kennedy notes that this was the case for many Irish companies at the time: 'Firms were forced to try to meet all orders and to produce a wide variety for a small market, so that there was little chance to specialise'.[76] In order to overcome this, in 1972, an almost textbook rationalisation programme was undertaken on the Marina. This was aimed at increasing productivity and improving the quality of the vehicles manufactured.

A view of the Marina in the mid-1970s. Note 'Dunlop House' in the middle of the photograph.
This building was constructed in 1966.

The rationalisation would see Cork become a 'two-car-line' – producing the two largest selling cars in Ireland, the Escort and the Cortina. These represented approximately 75 per cent of sales in the country at that time. In Irish commerce in general, the increasing concern with process technology and rationalisation plans crept in as a universal business practice in the 1970s, as trading conditions deteriorated.[77] Meanwhile, the Marina began exporting again and in the region of 4,000 vehicles were annually sent to Britain. The remaining units of the Ford range of vehicles were now imported from Britain, Holland and Germany.[78] The changes marked another historic move for Ford in Ireland to adapt to the changing market environment as presented. In 1982 Cork invested in the region of £10 million in modernising the plant for assembly of the Sierra and became a single-car plant.

Interior view of a section of the Parts and Accessories warehouse which was built on the Marina in 1967. Systemised numbering and storage of parts ensured rapid packing and despatching to Ford dealerships throughout the country.

There was buoyancy apparent as Ireland took her place in the EEC. However, the country's recent boom years were coming to an end. The impact of the oil crises of 1973 and 1979 were obviously significant for a country that depended on imports for almost three-quarters of its energy requirements. The knock-on effects on the balance of payments and inflation were severe and reflected, yet again, Ireland's susceptibility to external economic pressures.[79] In 1973 the registration of new cars and commercial vehicles went from 74,985 to 53,443 in 1975 and back up to 70,577 the following year, illustrating the rapidity with which things could change in the car world.[80] An interview with a former financial executive of Henry Ford & Son Limited noted that in: 'the car industry, you go from good times to bad times, very, very fast.'[81] The soaring fuel prices as a result of these crises furthermore dramatically changed motoring globally and a push towards smaller and more energy efficient vehicles became widespread.

Ireland's EEC accession would also have an impact on the scheme governing the assembly and importation of motor vehicles that had been negotiated in the previous decade. This clearly did not conform to the principles of free trade as espoused by the body. Safeguard measures for the motor vehicle assembly industry became an issue high on the priority list in the negotiations between the Community and the Irish delegation, led by Minister for External Affairs, Dr. P.J. Hillery.[82] A government publication particular to the motor assembly industry sums up the outcome of these deliberations in July 1971:

> As part of the arrangements for the transitional period of EEC membership a special twelve-year protocol was negotiated for the motor industry. This grew out of the recognition that motor assembly on the small scale prevalent in Ireland was unlikely to be viable in full free trade conditions. The aim therefore was to provide a breathing space during which the industry could maintain employment at the highest possible level while at the same time carry out the necessary steps towards diversification or specialisation which would provide longer run opportunities for profitable operations in competitive conditions.[83]

The efforts of Dr Hillery were a surprising breakthrough, after long and tense negotiations, but the bottom line was that from 1 January 1985, all quota restrictions on the importation of f.b.u. vehicles from any other country would be removed and the existing assemblers would be no longer obliged to assemble in order to import these vehicles, as was the existing arrangement.[84] It now became more apparent that the signature of a Corkman, Jack Lynch, endorsing Ireland's accession into the EEC would have serious consequences in his home city.

By 1977 the number of companies involved in the assembly of motor vehicles in Ireland had been reduced from the 1962 level of 22 to just fourteen.[85] However, there does not seem to have been any overt or immediate anxiety with regard to what lay ahead for Ford in Cork. In 1979 Henry Ford & Son Limited was commissioned with a very special project: the design and manufacture of a vehicle for a visit of Pope John Paul II.

Henry Ford II paid a visit to the Marina to mark the company's sixtieth anniversary in June 1977 and spoke optimistically of the future and made indications that there were plans evolving that could create 800 jobs in the not too distant future.

The Ford 'Pope-mobile' which was assembled in Cork in 1979.

The 'Pope-mobile' in the Phoenix Park during the Pope's Irish visit.

Certainly, we look at Ford of Ireland as a vital link in the Ford of Europe sales and manufacturing chain. That is why I see no reason for any reduction in the Cork plant's importance. Its role in our European plans has parallelled the emergence and strengthening of European economic co-ordination during the past ten years.[86]

His comments regarding Henry Ford & Son Limited were well greeted:

the almost 20,000 new Ford vehicles that we are building in Ireland this year create a continuing demand for Irish-made paints, glass, tyres and tubes, upholstery materials, batteries, lamp bulbs, and spark plugs that go into their assembly. I can't tell you exactly how many Irish jobs outside of Ford the supply of these Ford components represents. However, studies in the United States have shown that every automobile industry job has a 'multiplier effect' in creating up to six other jobs servicing or supplying motor vehicles or their users.[87]

While, obviously the backward linkages to the Irish industry were nowhere as great as those in the United States, yet Henry Ford & Son Limited was still vitally important in the demands it placed on many Irish businesses.

Henry Ford II addresses the workforce on the Marina in June 1977.

Henry Ford II, Paddy Hayes and Liam Cosgrave in 1977.

By early 1984, the clock was ticking. Rumours in a city the size of Cork quickly spread and it cannot have been encouraging to hear that the Dagenham foundry closing with a loss of 2,000 jobs.[88] There were now only three companies assembling motor vehicles in Ireland.[89] The 1985 deadline loomed closer and as it did Ford management anxiously looked for alternative options that might save the workforce from the unemployment queues that were lengthening at the time. None was forthcoming and on 17 January 1984 Paddy Hayes announced to the assembled 1,100 employees that production would cease towards the end of the year. The cocktail of influences; high domestic inflation; plant inefficiency and the inability to cope with free trade conditions were too much for the Marina. A total of 800 jobs would go which could be largely explained by the following description of one former Henry Ford & Son Limited financial executive:

> Quite apart from the inefficiencies of the very small plant we had here, what you were doing was, you were shipping the material in from Genk [Belgium] … and from Dagenham, into Ireland. You were making the stuff and then you had to ship the car back out again and ah, it made no economic sense quite apart from the fact … that we had labour inefficiencies here … OK, while our labour and overhead rate compared favourably with a German or a Genk or a Dagenham rate, by the time all the numbers were done … it just made no sense. And, of course, we were in the EEC then and … the tariff barriers went and there was no longer any requirement to have this proportion of home-built to imported units in place and really the economic justification of the plant was attacked on all fronts … In retrospect it's surprising it lasted so long.[90]

Further light is shed when the figures are placed side by side. At this time, the Genk plant was producing 1,400 Ford Sierras a day; Dagenham 1,000 and Cork a mere 80.[91] Cork carried losses of £25 million over the three years from 1980, with a further loss of £10 million in 1984. In corporate terms, this was simply not sustainable.

Considering the position and profile that the company had maintained in the country since its foundation in 1917, it would come as little surprise that discourse surrounding the Ford closure was expansive and intense. The economic climate, as it existed in the early 1980s, was one where the redundancy of so many skilled employees – in a city that had been proud of its unique Ford heritage spanning across eight decades – would easily dominate newspaper headlines. Interviews undertaken with former employees revealed that while many were totally surprised by the announcement, an almost equal proportion had clearly anticipated the demise of assembly – for the most part, on the basis of the economic position as outlined already. This variance is demonstrated in the answers to the general level of surprise at the contents of Paddy Hayes' speech: 'Not at all, no. There had been talk about it for years. And, from an economics point of view it was inevitable'.[92] Or the opposite:

there was nobody, but nobody guessed what was to come, and when that happened it came as a bombshell, I'm afraid, you know. And it sent shockwaves, not just through the assembled workforce, but I'd say through a lot of the … homes in Cork because a lot of these men, and you're going back now nineteen years … An awful lot of them never worked again.[93]

Some employees had less conventional suspicions that things were afoot:

And the first indication I knew was, I have to say this now, the men's toilet, the pipes weren't polished, you know the copper pipes. And they were meticulous about the company. They were always painting it inside and outside. Everything was meticulously clean – I'd say it was the cleanest plant, as such. But I saw where the pipes weren't 'brassoed' [polished] – I suppose to use the word – that was an indication. Yea, little things like that happening.[94]

There was a pretty general consensus that the cessation of assembly was not anticipated to come around quite as hastily as it ultimately did:

I think in general most people were surprised, like you know … not surprised- surprised at when it happened, they thought it would go longer.[95]

In retrospect, it is, in some ways, incredible that there was any palpable level of surprise in 1984 – especially considering the time-constrained nature of the arrangements that had been bargained by Dr Hillery. However, some comments put this point in perspective. One former director noted:

And we knew we'd close but nobody in Ireland believed that Ford would ever close. It just couldn't happen, they said. Ah, whatever about everybody else, Ford was there since 1917 etc., etc., etc., 'twill never close, but it did. And we knew that we'd have to close it. Because, to have the modern facilities of doing mass production, you had to have automation and you couldn't have automation unless you were doing about 200,000 units a year. We were doing much, much less than that.[96]

One lady who had spent her working career entirely on the Marina explained:

> I suppose, if you anticipate something and when it happens, the realisation is worse than the anticipation, as you know … it kind of really hits home.[97]

Another retired director, when questioned on this issue, was quick to note:

> We had conditioned the workforce, over two years, to what was happening. In other words, we didn't suddenly walk out on one January morning in 84 and say 'we're closing the plant'. They had been well aware that things were happening, even nationally, assembly plants here were closing up … It was still a shock and it was traumatic for all of us involved but it wasn't completely out of the blue … It was just economics.[98]

The observations of one political leader following the closure announcement are worth recalling:

> The leader of the Workers Party, Mr Tomas MacGiolla, couldn't understand all the expressions of shock and surprise because, he said, the terms of our entry to the EEC made it clear that protection would be removed for the industry by the end of 1984. Successive governments had failed to provide alternative employment in the industry for the past twelve years, he said, and in that time every other car assembly plant in the country had closed, with the loss of 12,000 jobs.[99]

It is a little eerie to note that the plant of Henry Ford & Son Limited closed its gates for the final time on Friday 13 July 1984.[100] There is little disagreement as to the enormous impact the Ford closure had on the city and ancillary industries. It was a stressful time for the economy and indeed the many families who were dependent on Fords in various ways. One man, whose job had survived the redundancies, explains how the cessation of production obliquely affected his own career. His assertions pinpoint an aspect that was at the very heart of Henry Ford & Son Limited existence over an extended period:

> I couldn't stick this, do you see. My job was production ran and now there was no production and I was bored to tears. And now I'd go out in the factory and there was nobody there, there was no one to shout at you, there was no one to say hello to. 'Twas unbelievable, 'twas frightening. 'Twas a very sad day. A terribly sad day to walk out to the factory where normally there'd be a buzz, there'd be working all people working

people passing up and down and you wouldn't walk from there to there without having some word spoken to you or some you know, jokes or remarks or something and I decided I'd go.[101]

*Aerial view of the Marina around 1970. Few would have anticipated
how much the Marina would change in coming years.*

The estimated annual loss in wages was £12 million locally and a further £22 million in purchases nationally.[102] A former director noted in interview that:

> the ripple effect outward was enormous, you know and it was very emotive as well because … there was guys there like, well into 40 years and they might have been second generation, and things like that, you know, the trauma on them was enormous, absolutely enormous.[103]

The Ford closure – along with the similar action taken by the Dunlop plant – brought the number of jobs lost in the city, since only September of the previous year, to at least 1,800 persons. In 1983 2,470 jobs were lost in the area and Cork unemployment rose by 21 per cent.[104] Suddenly, there was almost one million square feet of vacant factory floor space on the Marina and it was becoming clear that as trading conditions deteriorated 'the flexibility possessed by multinational enterprises to rationalise operations and close down marginal units found expression in Ireland in an increasing incidence of plant closures and at a significantly higher rate among foreign-owned enterprises'.[105] On this July day, after 67 years, a pivotal part of the city's twentieth-century history had reached its conclusion. The losses were great. Not just economically. With the closure, an entire part of the Cork community had also been wiped away:

> I haven't gone down to the plant since it stopped, no … It wouldn't be the same. This is now to me, ah the plant was the plant, it was the people inside it, it was the people inside it.[106]

Afterword

'I benefited from my experiences. After Fords, every work assignment, including two years
of active military service, was downhill'.
John Brennan, 1984 [1]

Not too long after I first came in contact with Henry Ford & Son Limited, I was made aware of an expression which gave the title to this book: 'Are you still below?' And, I will never forget the first time I was asked this. You see, over the course of my research, I became part of 'this particular type of Corkishness'. Despite mitigating factors (my relative youth and gender, the fact that I was not from Cork, that I represented the academe and that I knew next to nothing about either cars or the world that surrounds their manufacture, sales and distribution) even I had managed to etch a niche in this very specific Cork community.

Even today, when I enter the offices of Henry Ford & Son Limited at Elm Court, I feel like I am returning to a familiar place, to a sense of community, and in a way, to a type of home. With that in mind, I can empathise with the emotions of individuals who spent long periods working on the Marina, or those who had followed in the footsteps of family members. For some, like me to a much lesser extent, Fords had become a defining part of them.

I have to admit that I knew very little, practically nothing, about Fords when I started this project. I was young when the plant closed in Cork and I am pretty typical of most females in my general apathy towards the wonders of cars. But the story of Fords in Cork quickly reeled me in, for two important reasons. The first was Denis McSweeney, and more particularly how he so eloquently recounted memories, observations, jokes, nicknames and stories of life on the Marina. My appetite had been whetted. The second reason was the reaction of outsiders when I solicited opinions on Fords. Immediately, I noticed that often all that people wanted to talk about (by that, I mean those who had never worked there) was the plant closure.

It seemed to me that the almost seven-decade history of the plant had been reduced to narratives surrounding the events of 1984: and sometimes all that remained were passionate and angry criticisms of a multinational which had, as one eminent Cork historian vociferously informed me, 'disembowelled' Cork's economy by pulling out. Even back then, an assertion of this magnitude seemed too one-dimensional and I was becoming more and more interested in the reactions I was encountering on the subject.

With these issues in mind, I set out to write a history of the plant. The narrative is not to be seen as a corrective, while it may go some way in achieving this. Moreover, what I aspired was to provide a history which reflects the actual workings of the plant. I wanted to make personalities who worked there a central part of the analysis. I can only hope that the memories I have built into this history do justice to those who worked for Henry Ford & Son Limited. I worked with the documentary evidence I could locate and that which I could cobble together from the interview process. This may not be a narrative that will reflect the outlook of everyone, I have come to accept over time. The comments of one scholar seemed fitting in this context:

> Layered rather than literal, memory may be what is left over after dominant and subordinate, individual and group work out their version of what happened and why. It is never neutral or, for that matter, all encompassing. It is always selective because everything cannot be remembered anyway and because it serves the needs of all kinds of groups and individuals in thinking about where they have been and where they currently are.[2]

In New York, late in 2006, I serendipitously came across a Corkman; Ford identification holder 1103, who had worked in Henry Ford & Son Limited from 1948 into the early 1950s. His name is John Brennan. He declined my attempts to interview him and I was somewhat disappointed with that, as I was eager to hear the recollections of someone who had taken the migrant path after being laid off from the Marina. Instead, John promised to send me a piece he had written in 1984 on his memories of working in Fords.

As someone who prefers the intimacy of an oral interview, I was a little lethargic about the proposal to provide me with a written piece. That was until a package arrived on my doorstep, containing the over twenty-year-old article; John's recollections succinctly penned many of the characteristics of Fords I had written about. John's narration was so clear and was well-written; it was almost as if his memories had been distilled by his move from Cork so soon after leaving the Marina.

For most of the narrative, the author was quite critical of aspects of working life on a pre-unionised Marina but, in conclusion, he was also very grateful for having experienced such a beneficial induction into the reality of working. The encounter with John's reminiscences was, for me, very fruitful. I realised I could not hope to represent the perspective of every person who had worked for Fords and that the memories of Fords could be positive and negative, almost in the same breath. The relationship individuals have with their work place and colleagues varies from person to person and evolves over time.

In all, the history of the Marina provides a fascinating case study of a branch of a global conglomerate developing certain very local and specific characteristics over time. It is hoped that this book adds to our understanding of this unique chapter in Cork's twentieth-century history. In any case, as already noted, Henry Ford & Son Limited still exists as a company and in many ways its structure continues to adapt, as it did throughout the history of the plant. As one interviewee noted:

> It is an organism … a corporation of this magnitude … It is a living organism …
> It rolls on, I mean, it has an inevitability about it.[3]

What is clear is that this 'organism' left a mark which is still visible in Cork today. Henry Ford, I am sure, would be proud of this mark and his legacy.

Appendix i

Trade Unions in operation at Henry Ford & Son Limited[1]

1. Amalgamated Engineering Union
2. Amalgamated Society of Woodworkers
3. Cork House-Painters' Society
4. Irish Engineering Industrial and Electrical Trade Union
5. Irish Transport and General Workers Union
6. National Engineering Union
7. National Union Furniture Trade Operatives
8. National Union of Vehicle Builders
9. Plumbing Trade Union
10. Ship constructors' and Shipwrights' Association
11. The United Society of Boilermakers, Shipbuilders and Structural Workers

Appendix ii

Ford Cork's Tractor Shipments

1920			
British Isles	2152	Egypt	30
Bordeaux	214	Jaffa	5
Cadiz	388	Romania	100
Copenhagen	442	Turkey	5
Sweden	30	Asia Minor	10

1921			
British Isles	1241	Cologne	110
Bordeaux	50	Central Europe	40
Cadiz	2	Baghdad	24
Copenhagen	240		

1922			
British Isles	1290	Antwerp	150
Bordeaux	550	Reval	15
Finland	100	Copenhagen	75

Territory	1930	1931	1932	1933
Africa	55	-	1	-
Alexandria	2	-	30	-
Antwerp	158	102	79	3
Arcos-Russia	1	-	-	-
Asnieres	821	298	368	-
Australia	1009	25	-	-
Barcelona	321	29	70	-
Brazil	50	-	-	-
Buenos Aires	720	-	-	-
Canada	1328	6	-	-
Chile	10	-	-	-
China	32	-	-	-
Copenhagen	350	162	150	-
Cristobal	69	12	-	-
England	1253	443	1902	6
Figi	-	2	-	-
Germany	749	75	-	-
Helsingfors	146	101	43	-
Hanoi-French China	-	1	-	-
Havana	22	-	-	-
India	30	2	-	-
Irish Free State	93	73	63	57
Istanbul	387	44	27	-
Italy	695	279	2	-
Madagascar	-	-	1	-
Malaya	17	-	17	1
Malta	-	-	1	-
Mexico	65	-	-	-
Montevideo	33	-	-	-
New Zealand	60	-	-	-
Portugese E. Africa	-	1	-	-
Rhodesia	-	2	-	-
Rotterdam	53	82	43	-
Stockholm	322	96	250	-
U.S.A.	6446	1801	1	-
West Indies	-	3	-	-
Yokhama	75	-	-	-

Source: HFL, Acc 1, 'Production Figures', undated.

Appendix iii
Biographical Note on Sir Patrick Hennessy

'They used to call him St Patrick'[2]

'Just as the Cork factory was a showplace for the latest industrial techniques, so it proved the training ground for the talents of a number of outstanding young men who were to make their mark on Ford history.'[3]

Patrick Hennessy was born on 18 April 1898 in Midleton County Cork. His father, also Patrick, was a Roman Catholic who was a foreman on an estate.[4] His mother, Mary Benn – who was disowned on marriage – was the daughter of the Protestant owner of the estate on which Patrick (senior) worked.[5] Their son, Patrick joined Henry Ford & Son Limited in 1920 after war service as a Commissioned Officer with the Royal Inniskilling Fusiliers where -as one of the youngest serving officers – he spent the last ten months of the First World War in prison camps in Germany and Poland.[6] He would not be the only member of his immediate family to work for Ford: both brothers, Harry and William, would serve as 'Ford' men.[7] Patrick himself started on the shop floor in the foundry and worked in the blacksmith's forge, machine shop and on the assembly line[8] before being promoted to testing tractors as they came off the assembly line. The following year, 1921, he was transferred to England as a Road Representative for Ireland, but returned to Cork in 1923.[9] Patrick married Dorothy Margaret Davis of Boardmills in Northern Ireland in that year.[10] By 1929 he had been appointed Production Manager of the Cork plant. For the next two years, he engaged in developing the tractor business in Europe.[11] He was 'propelled into the limelight by a huge order for spare parts to service the 25,000 Fordson tractors in the USSR' in late 1928.[12] Hennessy's efforts saw the order being completed six months ahead of schedule. When Dagenham opened in 1931, he transferred there in the key role of Purchase Manager.[13] He held this post until 1939 when he was appointed General Manager. During the Second World War he was seconded from Dagenham to help Lord Beaverbrook at the Ministry of Aircraft Production, 'where his unique talents … were directed to co-ordinating materials requirements and working out a production plan for the entire aircraft industry to cope with the extraordinary demands of the Battle of Britain'.[14] Knighted in 1941 for his services at this time, by 1945 he was appointed a Director of Ford Motor Company Limited and became Managing Director three years later.[15] In 1956, Sir Patrick succeeded Sir Rowland Smith as chairman of Ford of Britain.[16] His long and varied experience in the motor industry was recognised in 1966, when he was elected President of the Society of Motor Manufacturers and Traders Limited. Two years later Sir Patrick retired from the chairmanship of Ford of Britain.[17] Having been appointed chairman of Henry Ford & Son Limited in 1955, he retired from this post in 1977 but he remained as a director until his death on 13 March 1981.[18] He was predeceased by his wife – with whom he had two sons and one daughter – in 1949.[19] His service to the Ford company, spanning seven decades, was an amazing record for a young man who had started in Cork's foundry in 1920.

Appendix iv
The Oral Interviews

As part of my compiling this history, Henry Ford & Son Ltd., in late 2002, invited former employees to participate in interviews aimed at bringing together their personal recollections of the firm. This formed part of larger projects aimed at commemorating the Ford Motor Company's centenary in 2003. I then contacted those who had agreed to participate directly and undertook the interviews over a period from late 2002 into the summer of 2004. Recollections stretch back to the late 1920s, although for obvious reasons more recent decades are better served; the positions held range from factory floor to senior management and directorship levels. Early on, I was struck by the acute awareness among senior management of life on the factory floor. I soon learned that this could be explained by three factors: the comparatively small nature of the Cork plant; the fact that many members of management had started their careers with the company at plant floor level; and, finally, the fact that family networks often extended throughout the Leeside organisation. This level of familiarity would be impossible in a larger works and was a unique feature of the Cork plant in Ford's global operation.

The interviewees were almost exclusively male. This gender bias is reflective of the work environment in engineering and vehicle production. It was a male-dominated factory where women were unrepresentative in manufacturing. The few women who did work in the Marina plant invariably held posts in administration or finance. The role of women in the workplace was entirely different to the standards of more recent times and the Ford workforce mirrored the status quo of its era. I also became mindful of the fact that I was a young woman interviewing mostly older men. On occasion I sensed that the language used and stories as told may have been modified with this in mind. Generally, the oral histories on the plant have revealed an under-researched aspect of Irish social history. The Public Relations Committee at Henry Ford & Son Limited decided in 1966 that 'some tape recordings should be made of veteran employee's recollections of the Company'.[20] It appears that this was overlooked in the preparations for the company's jubilee at that time. Many memories were undoubtedly lost since then, so in many respects the fieldwork undertaken here was a rescue operation. Nonetheless, this study will contribute towards gaining a greater understanding of the plant of Henry Ford & Son Limited and of life within it for those who worked there.

Endnotes for Appendices

1   SIPTU Cork, Branch 6 files: Henry Ford 1982-86 – 'Procedure Agreement between Henry Ford and Son Limited and Certain Trade Unions', 20 September 1965.

2   Bob Elliott interview.

3   *Ford in Ireland – The First Sixty Years 1917-1977*, p. 19.

4   David Burgess-Wise, 'Sir Patrick Hennessy' in David J. Jeremy (ed.), *Dictionary of Business Biography A Biographical Dictionary of Business Leaders Active in Britain in the Period 1860-1980* Vol. 3 (Butterworths, London, 1985), p. 165.

5   Ibid.

6   Roberts, *Ford. Model Y Henry's Car for Europe*, p. 17.

7   *Ford News*, June 1968.

8   *Ford in Ireland – The First Sixty Years 1917-1977*, p. 19.

9   HFL, Acc 2, 'News Release on Sir Patrick Hennessy', undated.

10   Burgess-Wise, 'Sir Patrick Hennessy', p. 169.

11   Ibid.

12   Roberts, *Ford. Model Y Henry's Car for Europe*, p. 17.

13   Ibid.

14   Hayes, *Henry. A Life of Henry Ford II*, p. 24.

15   HFL, Acc 2, 'News Release on Sir Patrick Hennessy', undated.

16   Roberts, *Ford. Model Y Henry's Car for Europe*, p. 17.

17   HFL, Acc 2, 'News Release on Sir Patrick Hennessy', undated.

18   Burgess-Wise, 'Sir Patrick Hennessy', p. 169.

19   Ibid.

20   HFL, Acc 2, 'Minutes of the Public Relations Committee Meeting', 16 June 1966.

Foreword

[1] In the early 1920s, Edward Grace, the MD at the Marina, was instructed to go to Britain to seek out a suitable location for a Ford factory. He selected a site at Dagenham, on the marshes of the Thames in Essex. Following the introduction of tariffs, arising from the economic war with Britain, much of the foundry activity, as well as the accompanying jobs at the Marina, was relocated to Dagenham.

[2] A term of contemptible endearment for the man on the production line, especially the more vocal members.

[3] Sarcasm of a quintessentially Cork variety.

[4] Marina workers who migrated with their jobs to Essex, to return each year for holidays and family reunions.

Preface

[1] Henry Ford (in collaboration with Samuel Crowther), *Today and Tomorrow* (Doubleday, Page & Co., New York, 1926), p. 263.

[2] HFL, Acc 2, 'Speech made by Henry Forda II', 1977.

[3] Walter Hayes, *Henry A Life of Henry Ford II* (Weidenfeld and Nicolson, London, 1990), p. 18.

[4] Kevin C. Kearns, *Dublin Voices: An Oral Folk History* (Gill & Macmillan, Dublin, 1998), p. 13

[5] Donnocha O Dulaing, *Donnocha Walking and Talking with Donncha O Dulaing* (Blackwater Press, Dublin, 1998), p. 55

Chapter 1: Why Cork

[1] Henry Ford (in collaboration with Samuel Crowther), *Today and Tomorrow,* (Doubleday, Page & Co., New York, 1926), p. 257.

[2] BFRC, Acc 266, box 1, C. Addison to Percival Perry (Ford Motor Company [England]), 28 June 1917.

[3] *Cork Examiner*, 8 August 1912.

[4] Results of these investigations are found in Ford R. Bryan, *The Fords of Dearborn: An Illustrated History* (Harlo, Detroit, 1987).

[5] Mira Wilkins and Frank E. Hill, *American Business Abroad. Ford on Six Continents* (Wayne State University Press, Detroit, 1964), p. 70. See also *Free State Farmer*, Vol.3, 1928, p. 13.

[6] Wilkins and Hill, *American Business Abroad,* p. 66.

[7] BFRC, Acc 1, box 105, Edward A. Rumley to Henry Ford, 13 June 1912. Rumley had sent Ford a copy of Ebenezer Howard's book and in his accompanying letter he listed some similar philanthropic ventures that Ford might visit during his 1912 European trip.

[8] See Frederick H.A. Aalen, *The Iveagh Trust: the first hundred years, 1890-1990* (Iveagh Trust, Dublin, 1990).

[9] NAI DT S5782B, MacWhite of the Delegation of the Irish Free State in Washington to Cosgrave, 19 May 1930.

[10] Louis M. Cullen, *An Economic History of Ireland since 1660* (Batsford, London, 1972), p. 167.

[11] Ibid.

[12] David S. Jacobson, 'The Political Economy of Industrial Location: The Ford Motor Company at Cork 1912-26', *Irish Economic and Social History,* Vol. IV (1977), pp. 39-40.

[13] Kieran A. Kennedy, Thomas Giblin and Deirdre McHugh, *The Economic Development of Ireland in the twentieth century* (Routledge, London, 1988), p. 8. See also David Johnson, *The Inter-war Economy in Ireland* (Gill and Macmillan, Dublin, 1973), pp. 20-1.

[14] Maura Murphy, 'The Working Classes of Nineteenth-Century Cork', *Journal of the Cork Historical and Archaeological Society*, Vol.LXXXV, No.s 241&242 (1980), p. 33.

15 Maura Murphy, 'Work and Workers in Cork City and County 1800-1900' in Patrick O'Flanagan and Cornelius G. Buttimer (eds.), *Cork History and Society Interdisciplinary Essays on the History of an Irish County* (Geography Publications, Dublin, 1993), p. 724.

16 Murphy, 'The Working Classes of Nineteenth-Century Cork', p. 33.

17 See any edition of *Guy's Trade Directory Almanac* and *Purcell's Almanac* from *circa* 1910 onwards.

18 D.J. Coakley (ed.), *Cork, Its Trade & Commerce – Official Handbook of the Cork Incorporated Chamber of Commerce and Shipping* (Guy and Co. Ltd, Cork, 1919), p. 62.

19 See Andy Bielenberg, *Cork's Industrial Revolution: 1780-1880, Development or Decline* (Cork University Press, Cork, 1991).

20 Edward P. Lahiff, 'Industry and Labour in Cork, 1890-1921', (MA thesis, University College Cork, 1988), p. 108.

21 Ibid, p. 109.

22 Coakley, *Cork: Its Trade & Commerce*, p. 62

23 *Ford Times*, March 1927, p. 301.

24 Jacobson, 'Ford Motor Company at Cork', p. 45.

25 For an historical look at aspects of the harbour see Mary Leland, *That endless adventure: a history of Cork Harbour Commissioners* (Port of Cork, Cork, 2001).

26 Coakley, *Cork: Its Trade & Commerce*, p. 62.

27 Ronnie Munck, *The Irish Economy Results and Prospects* (Pluto Press, London, 1993), p. 22.

28 Edward G.P. Brockie, 'The Rise of the Catholic Middle Classes in Ireland' (MA thesis, University College Cork, 1980), pp. 41-2.

29 In January 1914 the Ford Motor Company dramatically increased the minimum daily wage rate from $2.60 to $5. This applied to most of the company's 14,000 employees at the Dearborn location. See Stephen Meyer, *The Five Dollar Day: Labor Management and Social Control in the Ford Motor Company, 1908-1921* (State University of New York Press, Albany, 1981). Also William Simonds, *Henry Ford: a biography* (Michael Joseph Ltd., London, 1946), pp. 112-25.

30 *London Economist* is referenced as regarding the 'Five Dollar Day' as the greatest single step in the history of wages – See John B. Rae (ed.), *Henry Ford* (Prentice-Hall, Inc., Englewood Cliffs, NJ, 1969) p. 148.

31 Wilkins and Hill, *American Business Abroad*, p. 53.

32 Lahiff, 'Industry and Labour in Cork', p. 132.

33 Daniel L. Kelleher, *The Glamour of Cork* (Talbot Press, Dublin, 1919), p. 65.

34 Jonathan Houghton, 'The Historical Background', in John W. O'Hagan (ed.) *The Economy of Ireland: policy and performance of a small European country* (Gill & Macmillan, Dublin, 1995), p. 20. See also Cormac Ó Gráda, *Ireland: A New Economic History 1780-1939* (Clarendon Press, London, 1994), p. 380.

35 Ó Gráda, *Ireland: A New Economic History 1780-1939*, p. 382.

36 Jacobson, 'Ford Company at Cork', p. 45.

37 Ford, *Today and Tomorrow*, p. 258.

38 William Lewchuk, 'The Motor Vehicle Industry', Bernard Elbaum and William Lazonick (eds.), in *The Decline of the British Economy* (Clarendon Press, London, 1986), p. 144. See also Jacobson, 'Ford Company at Cork', p. 40.

39 See Andrew Boyd, *The Rise of the Irish Trade Unions 1729-1970* (Anvil Books, Dublin,1972), pp. 83-93.

40 Lahiff , 'Industry and Labour in Cork', p. 161.

41 Bob Montgomery, *An Irish Roadside Camera 1907-1918* (Dreoilin Press, County Meath, 2000), p. 37.

42 John Moore, *Motor Makers in Ireland* (Blackstaff Press, Belfast, 1982), p. 5.

43 Cornelius F. Smith, *The History of the R.I.A.C.* (RIAC, Dublin, 1994), p. 115.

44 Henry G. Tempest (ed.), *The Irish Motor Directory* (W. Tempest Publishers, Dundalk, 1907 and 1914/15 editions).

45 David S. Jacobson, 'The Motor Industry in Ireland', *Irish Economic and Social History*, Vol. XII (1985), pp. 112-15.

46 Lahiff , 'Industry and Labour in Cork', p. 103. 47 Ibid. 48 *The Irish Motor Directory*, 1915, p. 8.

[49] Coakley, *Cork: Its Trade and Commerce*, p. 158.

[50] Ibid.

[51] Coakley, *Cork: Its Trade and Commerce*, p. 62.

[52] Thomas A. Linehan, 'The Development of Cork's Economy and Business Attitudes 1910 – 1939', (MA thesis, University College Cork, 1985), p. 26-7.

[53] NAI S4427, 'Statement regarding New Customs Duties as affecting Henry Ford & Son, Limited, Cork', Edward Grace to the President's Office, 9 March 1923.

[54] Jacobson, 'The Ford Motor Company at Cork', p. 55.

[55] For the Cork perspective on this and Ford's arrival more generally see *Monthly Bulletin of the Cork Industrial Development Association*, Vol. I, No. 3 (March 1918), Eagle Printing, Cork, 1918.

[56] Wilkins and Hill, *American Business Abroad*, p. 69.

[57] E.J. Riordan, *Modern Irish Trade and Industry* (Methuen & Co. Ltd., London, 1920), p. 286.

[58] A concise account of the 'Peace Ship' episode is provided by Wilkins and Hill, *American Business Abroad*, pp. 63-4. See also Simonds, *Henry Ford: a biography*, pp. 125-40.

[59] *Motor News*, 3 March 1917, p. 317.

[60] Henry Ford (in collaboration with Samuel Crowther), *My Life and Work* (Doubleday, Page & Co., New York, 1925), p. 200 and p. 204. 'Drudgery' is the term that Henry Ford often used when referring to the difficulties of farming as an occupation.

Chapter 2: From a Green Field to a Great Foundry

[1] E.L. (Nobby) Clarke, who was manager of the Cork plant from 1926 to 1932, as interviewed on 'I remember Henry Ford', RTE Radio 1, 1982. Thanks to RTE for permission to use excerpts from this interview.

[2] *Ford Times*, March 1927, p. 301.

[3] Jacobson, 'Ford Motor Company at Cork', p. 37.

[4] Charles E. Sorenson, *My Forty Years with Ford* (Jonathan Cape, London, 1957).

[5] For tractor production figurres and the export destinations see Appendix (ii).

[6] Woodhead negotiated on Henry Ford's behalf with Cork Corporation and the Cork Harbour Commissioners – see Coakley, *Cork: Its Trade and Commerce*, p. 158. There is also an article on Woodhead contained in *Motor News*, 7 July 1917, pp. 988-90.

[7] Cork Improvement Act 1917 was passed on 10 July 1917. For a detailed breakdown of the Act and a history of the Park and Marina see G.M., 'Notes and Queries "The Cork Improvement Act, 1917"', *Journal of the Cork Historical and Archaeological Society*, Vol. 23, (1917), pp. 172-3.

[8] Hansard (Commons) 5th ser. XCI, 70, 7 March 1917.

[9] *Cork Examiner*, 21 February 1917.

[10] *Cork Examiner*, 1 March 1917. See also *Cork Constitution*, 1 March 1917.

[11] Riordan, *Modern Irish Trade and Industry*, p. 286. Linehan, 'The Development of Cork's Economy', p. 36. Jacobson, 'The Ford Motor Company at Cork', pp. 47-51.

[12] The contribution *Motor News* and *Irish Motor News* makes as a historical source is discussed by Finbarr Corry, *The Automobile Treasure of Ireland* (Dalton Watson, London, 1979), pp. 35-7.

[13] *Motor News*, 20 January 1917, pp. 78-9, 88, 96. *Motor News* 31 March 1917, p. 480. *Motor News*, 14 April 1917, p. 549. *Motor News*, 28 April 1917, pp. 621-6, 638.

[14] HFL, Acc 1, 'Henry Ford & Son Ltd. Estate Register', 26 September 1933.

[15] *Motor News*, 16 June 1917, p. 884.

[16] *Ford in Ireland The First Sixty Years 1917-1977* (Henry Ford & Son Limited, Cork, 1977), p. 12.

17 HFL, Acc 2, 'City of Cork particulars of the Marina Estate', 15 April 1962.

18 BFRC, Acc 65, box 9, 'Reminiscence of B.R. Brown Snr.', July 1955, p.17. Brown was later despatched by the company to oversee the building of the Ford plant in Japan.

19 Federico Bucci, *Albert Kahn: architect of Ford* (Princeton, Architectural Press, New York, 1991).

20 HFL, Acc 1, 'A Visit to the Works of Henry Ford & Son Ltd., Marina, Cork by J.C.P.', 1927, p.11.

21 BFRC, Acc 328, box 1, 'Minutes of Meeting of Directors', 8 July 1919.

22 Evidence of this is found in a recent biography of Terence MacSwiney where reference is made to his being solicited in the procurement of employment at Henry Ford & Son for a fellow nationalist. See Francis J. Costello, *Enduring the Most: the life and death of Terence MacSwiney* (Brandon Mount Eagle Press, Dingle, 1995), p. 122.

23 Peter Hart, *The I.R.A. and its enemies: violence and community in Cork, 1916-1923* (Clarendon Press, Oxford, 1998), p. 157.

24 HFL, Acc 2, 'Employee Records', undated. From these it can be seen that individuals who were former members of the British armed forces held a substantial portion of the management and supervisory positions in the early decades of the Cork plant.

25 *Cork Examiner*, 18 March 1920.

26 *Cork Constitution,* 30 October 1930.

27 Wilkins and Hill, *American Business Abroad*, p. 105.

28 BFRC, Acc 38, box 46, Port Stewart to Sorenson, 13 August 1920.

29 HFL Acc 1, 'Production Figures', undated.

30 BFRC, Acc 38, box 45, Grace to Donal O'Callaghan (Lord Mayor of Cork), 25 August 1921.

31 The road built became the later well-known Centre Park Road and was colloquially referred to as 'Ford's Road' for many years.

32 BFRC, Acc 38, box 45, Grace to Sorenson, 7 March 1922.

33 *The Irish Times*, 3 March 1922.

34 BFRC, Acc 38, box 45, Grace to Sorenson, 12 April 1922.

35 Wilkins and Hill, *American Business Abroad*, p. 106.

36 NAI DT S4427, Edward Grace to Arthur Griffith, 6 February 1922.

37 *Ford in Ireland. The First Sixty Years 1917-1977*, p. 17.

38 BFRC, Acc 6, box 47, 'Statement of Assets for Henry Ford & Son Limited', 31 July 1923.

39 NAI DT S4427, 'Statement regarding New Customs Duties as affecting Henry Ford & Son, Limited, Cork', Edward Grace to the President's Office, 9 March 1923.

40 *Motor News,* 17 November 1928, p. 1898.

41 *Cork Examiner*, 16 May 1930. See also noted in Henry Ford, *Moving Forward*, p. 264.

42 *Ford Times*, March 1927, p. 301.

43 E.L. (Nobby) Clarke as interviewed on 'I remember Henry Ford'.

44 *Evening Echo*, 3 August 1982.

45 Plunkett Carter, *A Century of Cork Soccer Memories* (Greenmount Rangers AFC, Cork, 1995), p. 15.

46 BFRC, Acc 65, box 9, 'Reminiscence for Mr. B.R. Brown Sr.', July 1955, p. 18-9.

47 Ford, *Today and Tomorrow*, p. 258.

48 E.L. (Nobby) Clarke as interviewed on 'I remember Henry Ford'.

49 NAI DT S5782B, MacWhite (the Delegation of the Irish Free State in Washington) to Cosgrave, 19 May 1930.

50 NAI DT S5782B, Coakley (Cork Incorporated Chamber of Commerce and Shipping) to Cosgrave, 12 March 1929.

51 Lahiff, 'Industry and Labour in Cork', p. 132.

52 The Ridgeway Estate was purchased in 1915 and the Milbrook Estate in 1916. Details in Wilkins and Hill, *American Business Abroad*, p. 66.

53 The Manchester plant had begun assembly in 1911. The establishment of the American motor interest in Britain is

outlined in Kenneth Richardson (assisted by C.N. O'Gallagher), *The British Motor Industry 1896-1936* (Macmillan Press, London, 1977), pp. 66-9.

[54] Wilkins and Hill, *American Business Abroad*, p. 137.

[55] *Ford Times,* May 1927, p. 455.

[56] Booton Herndon, *Ford. An unconventional biography of the two Henry Fords and their times* (Cassell, London, 1969), p. 15.

[57] The assembly had taken place on what was the world's first moving assembly line. This marked a watershed in modern manufacturing methods. A summary of the events surrounding this is provided by Alfred D. Chandler Jr., *The Visible Hand: the managerial revolution in American Business* (The Belknap Press of Harvard University Press, Harvard, 1977), p. 280.

[58] *Cork Examiner,* 30 December 1927, *Cork Examiner,* 31 December 1927, *Cork Examiner,* 4 January 1928. On all these days there were commentaries on the new Ford car production and its launch.

Chapter 3: The Dagenham Yanks

[1] *Cork Examiner,* 29 June 1963. John F. Kennedy is quoted from his speech made when receiving the freedom of the city of Cork.

[2] Patrick O' Sullivan (ed.), *Patterns of Migration, The Irish World Wide: History, Heritage, Identity,* Volume One, (Leicester University Press, London and Washington, 1992), p. xx.

[3] Henry Ford met the Trade Representative (Mr Dulanty) of the Irish High Commissioner's Office in London during this trip. See BFRC, Acc 38, box 56, Cosgrave to Ford, 18 November 1928. See also Wilkins and Hill, *American Business Abroad,* pp. 186 and 197.

[4] A contemporary account of the developments in Cork and Dagenham at this time are provided in the *Free State Farmer,* Vol. 3, No. 2, December 1928, p. 13.

[5] BFRC, Acc 38, box 56, Clarke to Sorenson, 26 November 1928.

[6] Wilkins and Hill, *American Business Abroad,* p. 205.

[7] *Ford Times,* May 1927, p. 455.

[8] HFL, Acc 1, 'Production Figures', undated. Note that a huge proportion of units produced in 1930 were carried out in the early part of the year, for example, in February alone there were 3,026 assembled.

[9] *Cork Examiner,* 16 May 1930 and *Cork Examiner,* 18 June 1930. Also alluded to in Wilkins and Hill, *American Business Abroad,* p. 228. Here they quote correspondence from Cork to Britain on 5 June 1930, stating 'We have had to lay off almost 6,000 men during the past three weeks ... which is a very serious consequence in a city of this size ... Naturally these men are all on the dole'.

[10] HFL, Acc 1, 'Production Figures', undated.

[11] The senior foreman in charge of the tractor assembly line was Jerry Keane who had moved with the company from Cork, see Gibbard, *The Ford Tractor Story,* p. 42.

[12] *Cork Weekly Examiner and Holly Bough,* 1954, p. 30. See also Sam Roberts, *Ford Model Y. Henry's Car for Europe* (Veloce Publishing Plc, Dorchester, 2001), p. 163.

[13] Enda Delaney, *Demography, State and Society. Irish Migration to Britain, 1921-1971* (Liverpool University Press, Liverpool, 2000), p. 173.

[14] Delaney, *Irish Emigration Since 1921,* p. 7.

[15] Davis, 'The Irish in Britain, 1915-1939', p. 20.

[16] Dominic Carey interviewed on 20 January 2003.

[17] The archive of *Ford News* retained by Henry Ford & Son Limited is an excellent source in tracking the careers of Cork workers. The information provided in the retirement notices and long-service awards clearly illustrates the pattern of lay-offs and spells spent working in the various British Ford locations.

[18] Delaney, *Demography, State and Society,* p. 171.

19 Enda Delaney, 'State, Politics and Demography: The case of Irish emigration, 1921-71', *Irish Political Studies*, No. 13, (1998), p. 34.

20 Eddie Cleary interviewed on 6 December 2002.

21 Joseph J. Lee, 'Emigration: A Contemporary Perspective' in Richard Kearney (ed.), *Migrations The Irish at Home & Abroad* (Wolfound Press, Dublin, 1990), p. 50.

22 Irish Centre for Migration Studies-'Breaking the Silence'- Stephen Barry.

23 Ultan Cowley, *The Men who Built Britain. A history of the Irish navvy* (Wolfhound Press, Dublin, 2001), p. 29.

24 Gus McLaughlin interviewed on 2 August 2003.

25 *International Labour Review*, Vol. 58, (Nov 1948), pp. 699-700.

26 John Healy, *No One Shouted Stop* (The House of Healy, Mayo, 1988), p. 45.

27 Eddie Cleary interview.

28 Sean Beecher, *The Story of Cork* (Mercier Press, Cork, 1971), p.104.

29 Irish Centre for Migration Studies – 'Breaking the Silence' – Patrick Devoy.

30 Tracey Connolly, 'Emigration from Ireland to Britain during the Second World War' in Andy Bielenberg (ed.), *The Irish Diaspora* (Longman, London, 2000), p. 61.

31 Wilkins and Hill, *American Business Abroad*, p. 328. See also Gibbard, *The Ford Tractor Story*, pp. 58-74.

32 HFL, Acc 1, 'Production Figures', undated. These indicate that production was suspended in Cork until early 1946.

33 NAI DT S5782B, O'Neill to Office of Minister for Industry and Commerce, 7 July 1941.

34 Delaney, 'Almost a Class of Helots in an Alien Land', p. 255.

35 Gibbard, *The Ford Tractor Story*, pp. 69-70.

36 Wilkins and Hill, *American Business Abroad*, p. 329.

37 Delaney, *Demography, State and Society*, p. 138.

38 John A. Jackson, *The Irish in Britain* (Routledge and Kegan Paul, London, 1963), p. 104.

39 Rex Pope, 'Metal, vehicle, and engineering industries' in Rex Pope (ed.), *Atlas of British Social and Economic History Since c. 1700* (Routledge, London, 1989), p. 55.

40 Huw Beynon, *Working for Ford* (Penguin, London, 1973), p. 45.

41 Ibid., p. 46

42 See Appendix iii.

43 *Cork Examiner*, 28 November 1950.

Chapter 4: Memories of the Marina

1 Denis Forde interviewed on 19 December 2002.

2 Alessandro Portelli, 'We're all on tape Voice Recording and the Electronic Afterlife' in Daniel Bertaux and Paul Thompson (eds.), *International Yearbook of Oral History and Life Stories, Vol. II, Between Generations: family models, myths and memories* (Oxford University Press, Oxford, 1993) p. 220.

3 HFL, Acc 2, 'City of Cork particulars of the Marina Estate', 15 April 1962.

4 Huw Beynon and Robert M. Blackburn, *Perceptions of Work: Variations within a factory* (Cambridge University Press, Cambridge, 1972) p. 39.

5 Ibid.

6 Denis McSweeney interviewed on 17 August 2004.

7 Paul Thompson, 'Playing at being skilled men: factory culture and pride in work skills among Coventry car workers', *Social History*, Vol. 13, (January 1988), p. 53. See also Bodnar, 'Memory and discourse in oral history: Autoworkers at

Studebaker', pp. 416-19.

[8] Arthur Owens interviewed on 27 November 2002.

[9] Many interviewees made reference to their serving under various managing directors.

[10] Arthur O'Callaghan interviewed on 27 January 2003.

[11] Denis McSweeney interview.

[12] Con Murphy interviewed on 6 December 2002.

[13] Oliver Barriscale interviewed on 28 November 2002.

[14] Tom Morrissey interviewed on 31 July 2003.

[15] Ibid.

[16] Pat Gillen interviewed on 21 January 2003.

[17] Oliver Barriscale interview.

[18] Paddy Hayes interviewed on 20 January 2003

[19] Denis Manning interviewed on 18 December 2002.

[20] Frank Dillon interviewed on 30 January 2003.

[21] Horace L. Arnold and Fay L. Faurote, *Ford Methods and the Ford Shops* (The Engineering Magazine Company, New York, 1915), p. 41.

[22] Bob Elliott interviewed on 22 January 2003.

[23] Ibid.

[24] Gus McLaughlin interview.

[25] Dominic Carey interview.

[26] Ibid.

[27] Gus McLaughlin interview.

[28] Steven Tolliday and Jonathan Zeitlin, 'Shop-Floor Bargaining, Contract Unionism and Job Control: An Anglo-American Comparison' in Steven Tolliday and Jonathan Zeitlin (eds.) *The Automobile Industry and its Workers Between Fordism and Flexibility* (Polity Press, Cambridge, 1986), p. 104.

[29] Arnold and Faurote, *Ford Methods and the Ford Shops*, p. 328.

[30] Ford, *Today and Tomorrow,* p. 260.

[31] Tolliday and Zeitlin, 'Shop-Floor Bargaining', pp. 99-120.

[32] Arthur O'Callaghan interview.

[33] Con Murphy interview.

[34] SIPTU Cork, Branch 6 files: Fords 1976-1983. This file contains numerous records of unofficial disputes.

[35] Tolliday and Zeitlin, 'Shop-Floor Bargaining', p. 104.

[36] Harry Shulman and Neil Chamberlain, *Cases on Labor Relations* (Foundation Press, Brooklyn, 1949), p. 434.

[37] Denis Forde interview.

[38] David Burgess-Wise, *Ford at Dagenham The Rise and Fall of Detroit in Europe* (Breedon Books Pub., Derby, 2001), pp. 92-3. See also Wilkins and Hill, *American Business Abroad*, pp. 332-3.

[39] Burgess-Wise, *Ford at Dagenham,* p. 92-3, April 21, 1982.

[40] SIPTU Cork, Branch 6 files: Henry Ford 1982-86-'Submission to the Labour Court on 1982, April 21, regarding the following claim from the unions'.

[41] SIPTU Cork, Branch 6 files: Henry Ford 1982-86- 'Procedure Agreement between Henry Ford and Son Limited and Certain Trade Unions', 20 September 1965. See also Appendix (i).

[42] Max Hayes interviewed on 5 December 2002.

[43] Ibid.

[44] Gus McLaughlin interview.

[45] Ibid.

[46] Paddy Hayes interview.

[47] Arthur Owens interview.

[48] Tom Morrissey interview.

[49] Ibid.

[50] Arnold and Faurote, *Ford Method and Ford Shops*, pp. 142-50.

[51] Ibid.

[52] Beynon, *Working for Ford*, p. 135.

[53] Tom Morrissey interview.

[54] Management Consultant Partners and Associates, *National Prices Commission Occasional Paper No. 26 Motor Vehicle Assembly Study* (Stationery Office, Dublin, 1978), p. 17.

[55] Ibid.

[56] Beynon, *Working for Ford*, p. 11-2.

[57] Denis McSweeney interview.

[58] O Dulaing, *Donnocha walking and talking*, p. 55.

[59] Studs Terkel, *Hard Times. An Oral History of the Great Depression* (New Press, New York, 2000 edn [1970]), p. 3.

[60] Michael J. O'Donoghue interviewed on 13 January 2003.

[61] Thompson, 'Playing at being skilled men', p. 57.

[62] Denis McSweeney interviewed.

[63] Derek S. Pugh and David J. Hickson, *Writers on Organizations* (Sage Publishers, California, 1997), p. 96.

[64] Tom A. O'Donoghue interviewed on 17 December 2002.

[65] Tom Morrissey interview.

[66] Frank Dillon interview.

[67] Gus McLaughlin interview.

[68] Tom A. O'Donoghue interview.

[69] Pat Gillen interview.

[70] Max Hayes interview.

[71] Arthur O'Callaghan interview.

[72] Thompson, 'Playing at being skilled men', p. 65.

[73] Max Hayes interview.

[74] Tom A. O'Donoghue interview.

[75] Billy Hurley interviewed on 5 December 2002.

[76] Elizabeth Tonkin, *Narrating Our Pasts: The Social Construction of Oral History*, (Cambridge University Press, Cambridge, 1992), p. 39.

[77] Some people consulted in the course of research remain working for Henry Ford & Son Limited presently.

[78] Noreen Kelly interviewed on 25 August 2003.

[79] Oliver Barriscale interview.

[80] Denis Forde interview.

[81] HFL, Acc 1, 'Henry Ford & Son Ltd. Estate Register'. Numerous leases dated from the 1930s and 1940s are held in this file. Leases were entered into by Fords with various companies from 1931 onwards. By 1938, sites and buildings belonging to Henry Ford & Son Limited housed, among others, Irish Dunlop Limited, Cork Gas Consumers Company, Irish Shell Limited, National Four Mills Limited and the Electricity Supply Board.

[82] Denis Manning interview.

[83] Denis McSweeney interview.

[84] Paul Thompson, *The Voice of the Past*, 3rd edn, (Oxford University Press, Oxford, 1978), p. 117.

[85] Bodnar, 'Memory and discourse in oral history: Autoworkers at Studebaker', p.442.

Chapter 5: The Cork Plant's Final Epoch

[1] Henry Ford, *Moving Forward,* (Doubleday Inc. Pub., New York, 1930), p. 49.

[2] *The Irish Times*, 19 January 1984.

[3] Houghton, 'The Historical Background', p. 22.

[4] Mary E. Daly, *Industrial Development and Irish National Identity, 1922-39* (Syracuse University Press, Syracuse, 1992) p. 32.

[5] Ibid., p. 40.

[6] Mike Cronin, 'Golden Dreams, Harsh Realities: Economics and Informal Empire in the Irish Free State' in Mike Cronin and John M. Regan (eds.), *Ireland: The Politics of Independence, 1922-49* (Macmillan Press, London, 2000), p. 156.

[7] *Ford in Ireland The First Sixty Years 1917-1977,* p. 29.

[8] Bob Montgomery, *Ford Manufacture & Assembly at Cork 1919-1984* (Dreoilín, Meath, 2000), p. 23.

[9] Ford, *Today and Tomorrow,* p. 259.

[10] Houghton, 'The Historical Background', p. 32.

[11] Cormac Ó Gráda, *A Rocky Road: the Irish Economy since the 1920s* (Manchester University Press, Manchester, 1997), p. 110.

[12] Ibid.

[13] HFL, Acc 1, 'Production Figures', undated.

[14] *Cork Examiner*, 9 September 1936.

[15] HFL, Acc 1, 'Production Figures', undated.

[16] Montgomery, *Ford Manufacture & Assembly at Cork,* p. 23.

[17] This marked the 25,000[th] car since 1932, not 1919.

[18] *Irish Motor News,* 21 April 1938, p. 141.

[19] *Cork Examiner*, 20 April 1938.

[20] *Cork Examiner* 10 September 1936. *Cork Examiner* 18 January 1938.

[21] HFL, Acc 1, 'Production Figures', undated.

[22] Mary E. Daly, *Social and Economic History of Ireland since 1800* (The Educational Company, Dublin, 1981), p. 157 .

[23] Ó Gráda, *A Rocky Road,* p. 110.

[24] HFL, Acc 1, 'Production Figures', undated.

[25] Frank Dillon interview.

[26] Arthur Owens interview.

[27] Con Murphy interview.

[28] NAI DT S5782B, O'Neill to Office of Minister for Industry and Commerce, 7 July 1941 and also referred to Denis Forde interview.

[29] Ó Gráda, *A Rocky Road,* p. 22.

[30] HFL, Acc 1, 'Production Figures', undated.

[31] HFL, Acc 1, 'Employee Records', undated.

[32] *Cork Examiner*, 9 February 1946.

[33] Ó Gráda, *A Rocky Road,* p. 11.

[34] HFL, Acc 1, 'Production Figures', undated.

[35] HFL, Acc 1, 'Employee Records', undated.

[36] *Cork Examiner*, 19 July 1950.

[37] Ibid.

[38] HFL, Acc 1, 'Production Figures', undated.

[39] Daly, *Social and Economic History of Ireland since 1800*, p. 159.

[40] Dominic Carey interview.

[41] Daly, *Social and Economic History*, p. 164.

[42] HFL, Acc 2, 'Export Summaries', undated.

[43] See Appendix (ii).

[44] *Cork Examiner*, 15 June 1953.

[45] *Cork Examiner*, 31 August 1954.

[46] *Cork Examiner*, 1 September 1954.

[47] *Cork Examiner*, 31 August 1954.

[48] *Cork Examiner*, 1 September 1954.

[49] Ó Gráda, *A Rocky Road*, p. 27.

[50] *Cork Examiner*, 12 October 1967.

[51] Dominic Carey interview.

[52] Paddy Hayes interview.

[53] NAI DTI, R312-223, 'Unemployment in Motor Assembly Industry', 22 June 1956.

[54] Ibid.

[55] Cullen, *An Economic History of Ireland since 1660*, p. 186.

[56] *Cork Examiner*, 12 October 1967 provides an outline of the new managing director's career with the company. He had started in the Cork plant in 1922 – at the age of sixteen – and progressed through the ranks, being transferred to Dagenham in 1932. There he would attain the position of Area Sales Manager before returning to Cork in 1955 as general sales manager before being appointed managing director.

[57] NAI DTI, CIO-2000/12/6, 'Committee on Industrial Organisation', 1961.

[58] Paddy Hayes interview.

[59] NAI DTI, CIO 76- 2000/12/38, draft copy of the 'Report on Survey of the Motor Vehicle Assembly', 1961, p. 4.

[60] Ibid.

[61] *Cork Examiner*, 14 June 1977. Contains an article with regard to the possibility of Ford's engaging in radiator fabrication.

[62] Houghton, 'The Historical Background', p. 36.

[63] D.J. Maher, *The Tortuous Path: the course of Ireland's entry into the EEC, 1948-73* (Institute of Public Administration, Dublin, 1986), p. 185.

[64] *Cork Examiner*, 12 October 1967.

[65] *Ford in Ireland. The First Sixty Years 1917-1977*, p. 34.

[66] *Cork Examiner*, 12 October 1967.

[67] Kennedy, et al., *The Economic Development of Ireland*, p. 68.

[68] *Cork Examiner*, 12 October 1967.

[69] Ibid.

[70] *Ford News*, January 1967.

[71] *Ford News*, February 1967.

[72] Arthur O'Callaghan interview.

[73] Hackett, *Ford in Europe*, p. 46.

74 Paddy Hayes joined the Cork Ford workforce in 1955 after graduating as a civil engineer. He progressed through working in production, the planning and drawing offices before ending up in production management. See 'Paddy Hayes – Mr Free Enterprise', *Business and Finance*, 26 April 1979, p. 6-7

75 Rex Pope, *The British Economy Since 1914: A Study in Decline* (Longman, London, 1998), p. 13.

76 Barry Brunt, 'The New Industrialisation of Ireland' in R.W.G. Carter and A.J. Parker (eds.), *Ireland. A Contemporary Geographical Perspective* (Routledge, London, 1988), p. 234.

77 Ibid, pp. 223-4.

78 *Ford in Ireland. The First Sixty Years 1917-1977*, p. 3.

79 Ibid, p. 37-9.

80 Lee Iacocca (with William Novak), *Lee Iacocca. An Autobiography* (Sidgwick & Jackson, London, 1984), p. 44.

81 Jim V. O'Donovan interviewed on 20 December 2002.

82 See D.J. Maher, *The Tortuous Path*, pp. 253-331. See also *The Irish Times*, 13 July 1971.

83 Management Consultant Partners, *National Price Commission Motor Vehicle Assembly*, p. 46.

84 *The Irish Times*, 13 July 1971.

85 Ibid, p. 15.

86 *Cork Examiner*, 14 June 1977.

87 Ibid.

88 *Cork Examiner*, 17 January 1984.

89 *Irish Motor Industry*, February 1984, p. 5.

90 Jim V. Donovan interview.

91 *Cork Examiner*, 3 January 1984.

92 Tom Morrissey interview.

93 Arthur O'Callaghan interview.

94 Pat Gillen interview.

95 Eddie Cleary interview.

96 Paddy Hayes interview.

97 Noreen Kelly interview.

98 John O'Callaghan interviewed on 18 August 2003.

99 *The Irish Times*, 19 January 1984.

100 *Cork Examiner*, 13 July 1984.

101 Tom A. O'Donoghue interview.

102 *Cork Examiner*, 13 July 1984.

103 Denis Manning interview.

104 *The Irish Times*, 19 January 1984.

105 Barry Brunt, 'Industrialisation within the Greater Cork Area' in Barry Brunt and Kevin Hourihan (eds.), *Perspectives on Cork* (Geographical Society of Ireland, Cork, 1998), p. 30.

106 Pat Gillen interview.

Afterword

1 John Brennan, ' Memories of Fords Cork', (unpublished article, courtesy of the author), 1984.

2 Bodnar, 'Memory and discourse in oral history: Autoworkers at Studebaker', p.414.

3 Denis McSweeney interview.

BIBLIOGRAPHY

Primary Sources

Ford publications and related material

Arnold, Horace L., and Faurote, Fay L., *Ford Methods and the Ford Shops*, The Engineering Magazine Company, New York, 1915

Barclay, Hartley W., *Ford Production Methods*, Harper & Brothers Publishers, New York, 1936

Ford, Henry (an authorised interview by Fay Leone Faurote), *My Philosophy of Industry*, Coward-McCann Inc., New York, 1929

_____ (in collaboration with Samuel Crowther), *My Life and Work*, Doubleday, Page & Co., New York, 1925

_____ (in collaboration with Samuel Crowther), *Today and Tomorrow*, Doubleday, Page & Co., New York, 1926

_____ (in collaboration with Samuel Crowther), *Moving Forward*, Doubleday Page & Co., New York, 1930

_____ *Things I've Been Thinking About*, Fleming H. Revell Company, London, 1936

Ford in Ireland The First Sixty Years 1917-1977, Henry Ford & Son Ltd., Cork, 1977

Ford in Europe the First Seventy Years, I.P.C. Transport Press, London, 1975

Hackett, Dennis, *The Big Idea the story of Ford in Europe*, Thomas Formand & Son Limited, Nottingham, 1978

Marquis D.D., Samuel S., *Henry Ford An Interpretation*, Little Brown and Co., Boston, 1923

Murray, Spence (ed.), *Ford in the thirties*, Petersen Publishing, Los Angeles, 1976

Official Publications

Coakley, D.J., *The General Principles of Housing and Town Planning*, Eagle Printers, Cork, 1917

_____ (ed.), *Cork: Its Trade and Commerce-Official Handbook of the Cork Incorporated Chamber of Commerce and Shipping*, Guy and Co. Ltd, Cork, 1919

Cork: A Civic Survey prepared by the Cork Town Planning Association, University Press of Liverpool and Hodder & Stoughton Ltd, London, 1925

Cork Incorporated Chamber of Commerce & Shipping, Report of the Council for the Year 1928, Purcell and Co., Cork, 1929

Donovan, Denis D., *Report on the Health of the City of Cork During 1910*, J. Mahony, Cork, 1911

Dunraven, The Right Honourable Earl of, *The Outlook in Ireland*, J. Murray, London, 1912

Fair Trade Commission, *Report of Enquiry into the conditions which obtain in regard to the supply and distribution of motor vehicles, tyres, other spare parts and accessories*, Dublin Stationary Office, Dublin, 1954

G.M., 'Notes and Queries "The Cork Improvement Act, 1917",' *Journal of the Cork Historical and Archaeological Society*, Vol. 23, (1917), pp.172-3

International Labour Review, Vol. 58, (Nov 1948), International Labour Office, Geneva, pp. 699-700

Irish National Productivity Committee, *The Irish Motor Trade, 1956-1965*, Irish National Productivity Committee Research Service, Dublin, 1965

Paper No. 26 Motor Vehicle Assembly Study, Stationary Office, Dublin, 1978

Nicholson, George F., *Cork Harbour Commissioners Complete Report and Comprehensive Plan for Development of Cork Harbour*, Purcell and Co. Printers, Cork, 1922

Riordan, E.J., *Modern Irish Trade and Industry*, Methuen and Co. Ltd, London, 1920

Tempest, Henry G. (ed.), *The Irish Motor Directory*, W. Tempest Publishers, Dundalk, 1907 and 1914/15 editions

Monthly Bulletin of the Cork Industrial Development Association, Vol. I, No. 3 (March 1918), Eagle Printing, Cork, 1918

Newspapers and Periodicals

Cork Examiner
Cork Constitution
Cork Weekly Examiner and Holly Bough
Evening Echo
Irish Times

Business and Finance
Ford News
Ford Times
Free State Farmer
Guy's Trade Directory Almanac
Irish Motor News
Irish Motor Industry
Motor News
Purcell's Almanac

Secondary Sources

Books and Articles

Aalen, Frederick. H.A., *The Iveagh Trust the first hundred years, 1890-1990*, Iveagh Trust, Dublin, 1990

Agar, Michael H., *The Professional Stranger An Informal Introduction to Ethnology*, Academic Press, San Diego, 1980

Andrews, Todd (C S.), *Dublin made me: an autobiography*, Mercier Press, Dublin, 1979

Baldwin, Neil, *Henry Ford and the Jews The Mass Production of Hate*, Public Affairs, New York, 2001

Ballard, Linda May, 'The folklorist and local history' in Gillespie, Raymond and Hill, Myrtle (eds.), *Doing Irish Local History Pursuit and Practice*, The Institute of Irish Studies, Queens University of Belfast, 1998, pp. 47-61

Gough, Michael, 'Socio-Economic Conditions and the Genesis of Planning in Cork', in Bannon, Michael J.(ed.), *A Hundred Years of Irish Planning (Vol. 1) The Emergence of Irish Planning 1800-1920*, Turoe Press, Dublin, 1985, pp. 307-32

Barrington, Ruth, *Health, Medicine & Politics in Ireland 1900-1970*, Institute of Public Administration, Dublin, 1987

Bartlett, Frederic C., *Remembering A Study in Experimental and Social Psychology*, Cambridge University Press, Cambridge, 1932

Beard, Charles A., *A Century of Progress*, Harper and Brothers Publishers, New York, 1933

Beecher, Sean, *The Story of Cork*, Mercier Press, Cork, 1971

_____ *Day by Day A Miscellany of Cork History*, Collins Press, Cork, 1992

Beiner, Guy and Bryson, Anna, 'Listening to the Past and Talking to Each Other: Problems and Possibilities Facing Oral History in Ireland, *Irish Economic and Social History*, Vol. XXX (2003), pp. 71-8

Boyd, Andrew, *The Rise of the Irish Trade Unions 1729-1970*, Anvil Books, Dublin,1972

Beynon, Huw, *Working For Ford*, Penguin, London, 1973

Beynon, Huw and Blackburn, Robert M., *Perceptions of Work Variations within a factory*, Cambridge University Press, Cambridge, 1972

Bielenberg, Andy, *Cork's Industrial Revolution: 1780-1880, Development or Decline*, Cork University Press, Cork, 1991

_____ *Locke's Distillery A History*, Lilliput Press, Dublin, 1993

_____(ed.), *The Shannon Scheme and the Electrification of the Irish Free State An Inspirational Milestone*, Lilliput Press, 2002.

Bodnar, John, 'Memory and discourse in oral history: Autoworkers at Studebaker', in Hofer, Tamas, and Niedermuller, Peter, (eds.), *Life History as Cultural Performance* (Budapest Ethnographic Institute of the Hungarian Academy of Sciences, Budapest, 1998), pp. 409-50

Bryan, Ford R., *The Fords of Dearborn An Illustrated History*, Harlo Press, Detroit, 1987

_____ *Friends Families and Forays Scenes from the Life and Times of Henry Ford*, Ford Books, Michigan, 2002

_____ 'Patrick Ahern, Henry Ford and Fair Lane', *Dearborn Historian*, Vol.22, No.1 (Winter 1982), pp. 3-12

_____ 'The Birth of the Ford Motor Company', *Dearborn Historian*, Vol. 23, No.1 (Winter 2003), pp. 7-25

Bracken, Damian and Nic Suibhne, Fionnuala, *University College Cork Oral History Project Handbook*, Unpublished Handbook, University College Cork, 1991

Braverman, Harry, *Labour and Monopoly Capital The Degradation of Work in the Twentieth Century*, Monthly Review Press, London, 1974

Brunt, Barry, 'Industrial and Harbour Development in Cork', *Irish Geography,* Vol. XII (1980), pp. 88-94

_____'Manufacturing Changes in the Greater Cork Area 1980-1984', *Irish Geography,* Vol.XVII (1984), pp. 101-8

_____'Industrialisation within the Greater Cork Area' in Brunt, Barry and Hourihan, Kevin (eds.), *Perspectives on Cork,* Geographical Society of Ireland, Cork, 1998, pp.19-37

_____'The New Industrialisation of Ireland' in Carter, R.W.G. and Parker, A.J. (eds.), *Ireland A Contemporary Geographical Perspective,* Routledge Science Paperbacks London, 1989, pp. 201-36

Bucci, Federico, *Albert Kahn: architect of Ford,* Princeton, Architectural Press, New York, 1991

Burgess-Wise, David, *Ford at Dagenham The Rise and Fall of Detroit in Europe,* Breedon Books Publishing, Derby, 2001

_____'Percival Lee Dewhurst Perry' in Jeremy, David J., (ed.), *Dictionary of Business Biography A Biographical Dictionary of Business Leaders Active in Britain in the Period 1860-1980,* Vol. 4, Butterworths, London, (1985), pp.639-43

_____'Sir Patrick Hennessy' in Jeremy, David J., (ed.), *Dictionary of Business Biography A Biographical Dictionary of Business Leaders Active in Britain in the Period 1860-1980,* Vol. 3, Butterworths, London, (1985), pp. 165-70

Butlin, Robin A., *Historical Geography Through the Gates of Space and Time,* Edward Arnold, London, 1993

Carter, Plunkett, *A Century of Cork Soccer Memories,* Greenmount Rangers A.F.C., Cork, 1995

Chandler Jr., Alfred D., *The Visible Hand the managerial revolution in American Business,* The Belknap Press of Harvard University Press, Harvard,1977

Chandler Jr., Alfred D., McCraw, Thomas K. and Tedlow, Richard S., *Management: past and present: a casebook on the history of American business,* South-Western College Publishing, Cincinnati, Ohio, 1996

Chart, David A., *An Economic History of Ireland,* Talbot Press, Dublin, 1920

Clancy, Mary, Clear, Catriona and Nic Giolla Coille, Triona (eds.), *Women's Studies Review Oral History and Biography,* Vol. 7, Women's Studies Center, Galway, 2000,

Cooke, Richard T., *My home by the Lee: The peoples' history of Cork,* Irish Millennium Publications, Cork, 1999

Cooke, Richard T., and Scanlon, Marion, *Cooke and Scanlon's guide to the history of Cork,* Modest Man Press, Cork, 1985

Colum, Padraic, *Cross roads in Ireland,* Macmillan, Dublin, 1930

Connerton, Paul, *How Societies Remember,* Cambridge University Press, Cambridge, 1989

Connolly, Tracy, 'Emigration from Ireland to Britain during the Second World War' in Andy Bielenberg (ed.), *The Irish Diaspora,* Longman, London, 2000, p.51-64

Corry, Finbarr, *The Automobile Treasure of Ireland,* Dalton Watson, London, 1979

Costello, Francis J., *Enduring the Most the life and death of Terence MacSwiney,* Brandon Mount Eagle Press, Dingle, 1995

Cowley,Ultan, *The men who built Britain: a history of the Irish navvy,* Wolfound Press, Dublin, 2001

Cramer, Tim, *The Life of Other Days,* Collins Press, Cork, 1992

Cronin, Mike, 'Golden Dreams, Harsh Realities: Economics and Informal Empire in the Irish Free State' in Cronin, Mike and Regan, John M., (eds.), *Ireland: The Politics of Independence, 1922-49,* Macmillan Press, London, 2000, pp.144-63

Cronin, Maura, *Country, Class or Craft? The Politicisation of the Skilled Artisan in Nineteenth-Century Cork,* Cork University Press, Cork, 1994

_____'From the 'Flat o' the city' to the Top of the Hill: Cork since 1700' in Clarke, Howard B. (ed.), *Irish Cities,* Mercier Press, Cork, 1995, pp. 55-68

_____'Work and Workers in Cork City and County 1800-1900' in O'Flanagan, Patrick and Buttimer, Cornelius G. (eds.), *Cork History and Society Interdisciplinary Essays on the History of an Irish County ,* Geography Publications, Dublin, 1993, pp.721-58

Crowley, Jimmy, *Jimmy Crowley's Irish Song Book,* Mercier Press, Cork, 1986

Cullen, Bill, *It's a Long way from Penny Apples,* Mercier Press, Cork, 2001

Cullen, Louis M., *An Economic History of Ireland since 1660,* Batsford, London, 1972 _____(ed.), *The Formation of the Irish Economy,* Mercier Press, Cork, 1969

D'Alton, Ian, 'Keeping faith: an evocation of the Cork Protestant Character, 1820-1920' in O'Flanagan, Patrick and Buttimer, Cornelius G., *Cork History and Society Interdisciplinary Essays on the History of an Irish County,* Geography Publications, Dublin, 1993, pp.759-92

Daly, Mary E., *Industrial Development and Irish National Identity 1922-1939,* Syracuse University Press, Syracuse, 1992

_____*Social and Economic History of Ireland since 1800,* Educational Company, Dublin, 1981

_____'An Alien Institution? Attitudes towards the City in Nineteenth and Twentieth Century Irish Society', *Études Irlandaises,* No. 10, (December 1985), pp.181-94

_____'Social structure of the Dublin working class, 1871-1911', *Irish Historical Studies,* Vol. XXIII, No. 90, (November,1982), pp.121-33

Davis, Graham, 'The Irish in Britain, 1915-1939', in Andy Bielenberg (ed.), *The Irish Diaspora,* (Longman, London, 2000), pp.19-36

De Barra, Eibhlis, *Bless 'em all: the lanes of Cork,* Mercier Press, Cork, 1997

Delaney, Teddy, *Where We Sported and Played Confessions of a Cork Boy,* Mercier Press, Cork, 1990

Delaney, Enda, *Irish Emigration Since 1921,* Dundalgen Press, Dublin, 2002

_____*Demography, State and Society Irish Migration to Britain, 1921-1971,* Liverpool University Press, Liverpool, 2000

_____'"Almost a Class of Helots in an Alien Land": The British State and Irish Immigration, 1921-45' in MacRaild, Donald M., (ed.), *The Great Famine and Beyond Irish Migrants in Britain in the Nineteenth and Twentieth Centuries,* Irish Academic Press, Dublin, 2000, pp.240-65

_____'State, Politics and Demography: The case of Irish emigration, 1921-71', *Irish Political Studies,* No. 13, (1998), pp.25-49

Dennison, Stanley R. and MacDonagh, Oliver, *Guinness 1886-1939 From Incorporation to the Second World War,* Cork U.P., 1998

Dunne, Catherine, *An Unconsidered People The Irish in London,* New Island, Dublin, 2003

Dunne, Sean (ed.), *The Cork Anthology,* Cork University Press, Dublin, 1993

Ellis, Peter Beresford, *A History of the Irish Working Class,* Gollancz , London, 1972

Fahy, Angela M., 'Place and Class in Cork' in O'Flanagan, Patrick and Buttimer, Cornelius G. (eds.), *Cork History and Society Interdisciplinary Essays on the History of an Irish County,* Geography Publications, Dublin, 1993, pp. 699-720

Ford, Percy, and Ford, Grace, *A Brevite of Parliamentary Papers 1900-1916,* Basil Blackwell, Oxford, 1957

Ford Ruddiman, Margaret, 'Memories of My Brother Henry Ford', *Michigan Historical Commision,* (September 1953), pp. 225-75

Foster OSM, Steward, *History of the Diocese of Brentwood,* The Diocese of Brentwood, Essex, 1994

Gibbard, Stuart, *The Ford Tractor Story: Dearborn to Dagenham 1917-64 Part 1,* Old Pond Publishing and Japonica Press, Driffield and Ipswich, 1998

Girvin, Brian, *Between Two Worlds Politics and Economy in Independent Ireland,* Gill and Macmillan, Dublin, 1989

Girvin, Brian and Roberts, Geoffrey (eds.), *Ireland and the Second World War: Politics, Scoiety and Remembrance,* Four Courts Press, Dublin, 2000

Glynn, Sean, 'Irish Immigration to Britain, 1911-1951: Patterns and Policy', *Irish Economic and Social History,* Vol.VIII, (1981), pp.50-69

Greenleaf, William, *Monopoly on Wheels Henry Ford and the Selden Automobile Patent,* Wayne State University Press, Detroit, 1961

Hammond, Roy, *Media Memories of Cork,* Leprechaun Productions, Cork, 1994

Hart, Peter, *The I.R.A. and its Enemies: violence and community in Cork, 1916-1923,* Clarendon Press, Oxford,1998

Hayes, Walter, *Henry A Life of Henry Ford II ,* Weidenfeld and Nicolson, London, 1990

Healy, John, *No one shouted stop!,* The House of Healy, Mayo, 1988

Hector, Michael, *Internal Colonialism, The Celtic Fringe in British National Development, 1936-1966,* Routledge and Kegan Paul, London, 1975

Hedges, Nick and Beynon, Huw, *Born to Work Images of Factory Life,* Pluto Press, London, 1982

Heenan, John C., *Not the Whole Truth*, Hodder and Stoughton, London, 1971

Henige, David, *Oral Historiography*, Longman, London, 1982

Hennessy, Jeremy, 'The man who introduced Ford to Ireland', *Motoring Life*, (May 1971), pp. 14-5

Herndon, Booten, *Ford An Unconventional biography of the two Henry Fords and their times*, Cassell, London, 1970

Hobsbawn Eric J., *Labouring Men Studies in the History of Labour*, Weidenfeld and Nicolson, London, 1968 edn (1964)

Hollingsworth, Thomas H., *Historical Demography*, Hodder and Stoughton, London, 1969

Holmes, Colin, *John Bull's Island*, Macmillan, London, 1988

Houghton, Johnathan, 'The Historical Background', in O'Hagan, John W., (ed.) *The Economy of Ireland policy and performance of a small European country*, Gill & Macmillan, Dublin, 1995, pp.1-48

Hourihan, Kevin, 'The Evolution and Influence of Town Planning in Cork' in O'Flanagan, Patrick and Buttimer, Cornelius G.(eds.), *Cork History and Society Interdisciplinary Essays on the History of an Irish County*, Geography Publications, Dublin, 1993, pp. 699-720

Hunter, Stephen (ed.), *Life Journeys Living in Ireland today*, Northside Folklore Project, Cork, 1999

Iacocca, Lee (with William Novak), *Lee Iacocca An Autobiography*, Sidgwick & Jackson, London, 1984

Jacobson, David S., 'The Political Economy of Industrial Location: The Ford Motor Company at Cork 1912-1926' in *Irish Economic and Social History*, Vol. IV, (1977), pp.36-55

_____ 'The Motor Industry in Ireland', *Irish Economic and Social History*, Vol.XII, (1985), pp.109-16

Jackson, John A., *The Irish in Britain*, Routeldge and Kegan Paul, London, 1963

Johnson, David, *The Interwar Economy in Ireland*, Economic and Social History Society of Ireland, Dublin, 1985

_____ 'The Economic History of Ireland between the Wars', *Irish Economic and Social Review*, Vol. I, 1974, pp. 49-61

Katz, Fred E., 'Integrative and adaptive uses of autonomy: worker autonomy in factories', in Salaman, Graeme and Thompson, Kenneth (eds.), *People and Organisations*, Longman, London, 1973

Kearns, Kevin C., *Dublin Street Life and Lore An Oral History*, Glandale Press, Dublin, 1991

_____ *Dublin Tenement Life An Oral History*, Gill and Macmillan, Dublin, 1994

_____ *Dublin Pub Life and Lore*, Gill and Macmillan, Dublin, 1996

_____ *Dublin Voices An Oral Folk History*, Gill and Macmillan, 1998

Kelleher, Daniel L., *The Glamour of Cork*, Talbot Press, Dublin, 1919

Kenneally, Christy, *Maura's Boy a Cork Childhood*, Mercier Press, Cork, 1996

Kennedy, Kieran A., Giblin, Thomas, and McHugh, Deirdre, *The Economic Development of Ireland in the twentieth century*, Routledge, London, 1988

Kennedy, Liam, *The modern industrialisation of Ireland: 1940-1988*, Dundalgan, Dundalk, 1989

Keogh, Dermot, *The Rise of the Irish Working Class The Dublin Trade Union Movement and Labour Leadership 1890-1914*, Appletree Press, Belfast, 1982

Kunstler, Howard, *The geography of nowhere: the rise and decline of America's man-made landscape*, Simon & Schuster, New York, 1993

Lacy, Robert, *Ford the Men and the Machine*, Heinemann, London, 1986

Lee, Joseph J., *The Modernisation of Irish Society 1848-1918*, Gill and Macmillan, Dublin, 1989 edn (1973)

_____ 'Emigration: A Contemporary Perspective' in Richard Kearney (ed.), *Migrations The Irish at Home & Abroad*, Wolfound Press, Dublin, 1990, pp. 33-44

Lee, Stephen, J., *Aspects of British Political History*, Routledge Books, London, 1996

Leffingwell, Randy, *Ford Farm Tractors*, MBI Publishing, Wisconsin, 1998

Leland, Mary, *That endless adventure: a history of Cork Harbour Commissioner*, Port of Cork, Cork, 2001

Lewchuk, William, 'The Motor Vehicle Industry', in Elbaum, Bernard. and Lazonick, William.(eds.), *The Decline of the British Economy*, Clarendon Press, London, 1986, pp. 135-61

Lewis, Roy and Maude, Angus, *The English Middle Classes*, Penguin, London, 1953

Lichtenstein, Nelson, 'Life at the Rouge: A Cycle of Workers' Control' in Stephenson, Charles and Asher, Robert (eds.), *Life and Labor Dimensions of American Working-Class History*, State University of New York, Albany, 1986, pp. 237-59

Lichenstein, Nelson and Meyer, Stephen, (eds.), *On the Line Essays in the History of Auto Work*, University of Illinois Press, Urbana, 1989

Lochner, Louis P., *America's Don Quixote: Henry Ford's attempt to save Europe*, Kegan Paul, Trench, Trubner, London, 1924

Lyons, Francis S.L., *Ireland Since the Famine*, Fontana Press, London, 1971

MacAmhlaigh, Donall (translated by Iremonger, Valentin), *An Irish Navvy: the diary of an Exile*, Routledge and Kegan Paul, London, 1964

MacSweeney, Rev. A.M., 'A Study of Poverty in Cork City', *Studies*, Vol. IV, (1915), pp.93-104

Management Consultant Partners and Associates, *National Prices Commission Occasional Papers No. 26* Motor Vehicle Assembly Study, Stationery Office, Dublin, 1978.

Maguire, Martin, 'A Socio-Economic Analysis of the Dublin Protestant Working Class, 1870-1926' in *Irish Economic and Social History*, Vol. XX, (1993), pp. 35-61

Maher, D.J., *The Tortuous Path: the course of Ireland's entry into the EEC, 1948-73*, Institute of Public Administration, Dublin, 1986

Manseragh, Nicholas, *The Irish Question 1840-1921*, George Allen and Unwin Ltd., London, 1965

McCarthy, Mark, 'Changes in Attitudes to Cities and Towns in Ireland: The Case of the Historical Research Community', *Chimera*, UCC Geographical Society, No. 12, (1997), pp. 78-90

_____ 'Researching Cork's Past: A Review of the Literature', *Chimera*, UCC Geographical Society, No. 14, (1999), pp.109-17

McElligot, Tom, *Six O' Clock All Over Cork*, Wolfhound Press, Dublin, 1992

McNamara, Tony F., *Portrait of Cork*, Watermans, Cork, 1981

Meenan, Prof. James, 'From Free Trade to Self-Sufficiency' in MacManus, Francis (ed.), *The Yeats of the Great Test*, Mercier Press, Cork, 1967

Messenger, Betty, *Picking Up the Linen Threads*, Blackstaff Press, Belfast, 1978

Meyer III, Stephen, *The Five Dollar Day*, State University of New York Press, Albany, 1981

Modell, Judith and Hinshaw, John, 'Male Work and Mill Work Memory and Gender in Homstead, Pennsylvania' in the *International Yearbook of Oral History and Life Stories Volume IV Gender and Memory*, Lyydesdorff, Selma, Passerini, Luisa and Thompson, Paul (eds.) Oxford Univeristy Press, 1996, pp. 133-49

Montgomery, Bob, *An Irish Roadside Camera Ireland's Earliest Motorists and their Automobiles 1896-1906*, Marino Books, Dublin, 1997

_____ *Ford Manufacture and Assembly at Cork 1919-1984*, Dreloin Press, County Meath, 2000

_____ *An Irish Roadside Camera 1907-1918*, Dreoilin Press, County Meath, 2000

Moore, John, *Motor Makers in Ireland*, Blackstaff Press, Belfast, 1982

Muldowney, Mary , 'A world on its own: recollections of women workers in Guinness's brewery in the 1940s', *Journal of the Irish Labour History Society Saothar*, (1998), pp.103-17

Murphy, Maura, 'The Working Classes of Nineteenth Century Cork' in *Journal of the Cork Historical and Archaeological Society*, Vol.LXXXV, No.241&242, (Jan-Dec 1980), pp.26-51

Munck, Ronnie, *The Irish Economy Results and Prospects*, Pluto Press, London, 1993

Nevins, Allan, *Ford the Times, the Man, the Company*, Charles Scribner's Sons, New York, 1954

Nowlan, Kevin B. (ed.), *Travel and Transport in Ireland*, Gill and Macmillan, Dublin, 1973

Nye, David E., *Henry Ford "Ignorant Idealist"*, Kennikat Press, London, 1979

O' Beirne, Gerald, *Siemens in Ireland 1925-2000 Seventy-five Years of Innovation*, A & A Farmar, Dublin, 2000

O'Brien, John B., 'Population, Politics and Society, Cork, 1780-1900' in O'Flanagan, Patrick and Buttimer, Cornelius G.(eds.), *Cork History and Society Interdisciplinary Essays on the History of an Irish County*, Geography Publications, Dublin, 1993, pp. 699-720

O'Brien, Joseph V., *"Dear Dirty Dublin" A City in Distress, 1899-1916*, University of California Press, London, 1982

O'Callaghan, Antoin, *The Lord Mayors of Cork 1900 to 2000*, Inversnaid Publications, Cork, 2000

O'Connor, Kevin, *The Irish in Britain*, Sidgwick and Jackson, London, 1972

O'Donovan, John, *Wheels and Deals People and Places in Irish Motoring*, Gill and Macmillan, Dublin, 1983

Ó Drisceoil, Diarmuid and Ó Drisceoil, Donal, *The Murphy's Story: the History of Lady's Well Brewery, Cork*, Murphy's Brewery, Cork, 1997

Ó Dulaing, Donnocha, *Donnocha walking and talking with Donncha O Dulaing*, Blackwater Press, Dublin, 1998

Ó Gráda, Cormac, *Ireland: a new economic history 1780-1939*, Clarendon Press, London, 1994

_____*A Rocky Road the Irish Economy since the 1920s*, Manchester University Press, Manchester, 1997

O' Mahony, Colman, *In the Shadows Life in Cork 1750-1930*, Tower Books, 1997

O' Mahony, David, *The Irish Economy*, Cork University Press, Cork, 1964

O' Mahony, Timothy, *Glimpses of Blackrock*, D.C. Graphics, Cork, 1985

Ó Murchadha, Diarmuid, *Liam De Roiste*, Dundalgan Press, Dublin, 1976

O'Sullivan, Patrick (ed.), *Patterns of Migration, The Irish World Wide: History, Heritage, Identity*, Volume One, Leicester University Press, London and Washingon, 1992

Passerini, Luisa, (translated by Lumley, Robert and Bloomfield, Jude) *Fascism in Popular Memory: the cultural experience of the Turin working class*, Cambridge University Press, Cambridge, 1986

Pettit, Sean, *My city by the Lee*, Studio Publications, Cork, 1987

Pope, Rex, 'Metal, vehicle, and engineering industries' in Pope, Rex (ed.), *Atlas of British Social and Economic History Since c.1700*, Routledge, London, 1989, pp.45-67

Plummer, Alfred, *International Combines in Modern Industry*, Routledge Thoemmes Press, London , 1934

Portelli, Allesandro, 'Oral History in Italy', in Dunaway, David K., and Baum, Willa K., (eds.), *Oral History: An Interdisciplinary Anthology* 2nd edn, Alta Mira Press, London, 1996, pp. 391-416

_____'We're all on tape Voice Recording and the Electronic Afterlife' in Bertaux, David and Thompson, Paul (eds.), *International Yearbook of Oral History and Life Stories, Vol. II, Between Generations: family models, myths and memories*, Oxford University Press, Oxford,1993, pp.217-21

Prunty, Jacinta, *Dublin Slums, 1800-1925 A Study in Urban Geography*, Irish Academic Press, 1999

Pugh, Derek S., and Hickson, David J., *Writers on Organizations*, Sage Publishers, California, 1997

Rae, John B., *The American Automobile Industry*, Twayne Publishers, Boston, 1984

_____*The American Automobile A brief history*, University of Chicago Press, Chicago, 1965

_____*Harry Ferguson and Henry Ford*, Ulster Historical Foundation, Belfast, 1981

_____(ed.), *Henry Ford*, Prentice-Hall, Inc., Englewood Cliffs, NJ, 1969

Rahilly, Alfred J., 'The Social Problem in Cork' in *Studies*, Vol. VI, 1917, pp.77-88

Richardson, Kenneth, (assisted by O'Gallagher, C.N.,), *The British Motor Industry 1896-1936*, Macmillan Press, London, 1977

Roberts, Sam, *Ford Model Y Henry's Car for Europe*, Veloce Publishing Plc, Dorchester, 2001

Shulman, Harry and Chamberlain, Neil, *Cases on Labor Relations*, Foundation Press, Brooklyn, 1949

Silverman, Marylin and Gulliver, Philip H. (eds.) *Approaching the Past Historical Anthropology through Irish Case Studies*, Columbia University Press, New York, 1992

Simonds, William, *Henry Ford: a biography*, Michael Joseph Ltd., London, 1946

Sinclair, Upton, *The Fliver King: A Story of Ford-America*, Charles H. Kerr Publishing Co., Chicago, 1984 edn (1937)

Smith, Cornelius F., *The History of the R.I.A.C.*, RIAC, Dublin, 1994

Smyth, William J., 'Explorations of Place' in Lee, Joseph, *Ireland towards a sense of place*, Cork University Press, Cork, 1985

Sorenson, Charles E., *Forty Years with Ford*, Johnathan Cape, London, 1957

Spradley, James P., *Participant Observation*, Holt Rinehart and Winston, New York, 1980

Sward, Keith, *The Legend of Henry Ford*, Atheneum, New York, 1968

Terkel, Studs, *Hard Times An Oral History of the Great Depression*, New Press, New York, 2000 edn (1970)

Thompson, Edward P., *The Making of the English Working Class*, Gollancz, London, 1965

Thompson, Paul, *The Nature of Work an introduction to debates on labour process*, Macmillan Press, London, 1983

_____ *The Edwardians*, Weidenfeld and Nicolson, London, 1975

_____ *The Voice of the Past Oral History*, 3rd edn, Oxford University Press, Oxford, 2000 edn (1978)

_____ 'Oral History in Italy', in Dunaway, David K. and Baum, Willa K., (eds.), *Oral History: An Interdisciplinary Anthology*, 2nd edn, Alta Mira Press, London, 1996, pp. 351-62

_____ 'Playing at being skilled men: factory culture and pride in work skills among Coventry car workers', *Social History*, Vol. 13, No., 1, (January 1988), pp.45-69

Tobin, Fergal, *The Best of Decades Ireland in the 1960s,* Gill and Macmillan, Dublin, 1984

Tolliday, Steven, 'Management and Labour in Britain 1896-1939', in Tolliday, Steven and Zeitlin, Johnathan (eds.), *The Automobile Industry and its Workers Between Fordism and Flexibility*, Polity Press, Cambridge, 1986, pp.29-56

Tolliday, Steven and Zeitlin, Johnathan, 'Shop-Floor Bargaining, Contract Unionism and Job Control: An Anglo-American Comparison' in Tolliday, Steven and Zeitlin, Johnathan (eds.), *The Automobile Industry and its Workers Between Fordism and Flexibility*, Polity Press, Cambridge, 1986, pp. 99-120

Tonkin, Elizabeth, *Narrating our Pasts the social construction of oral history,* Cambridge University Press, Cambridge, 1992

Walker, Charles R., and Guest, Robert H., *The Man on the Assembly Line*, Harvard University Press, Cambridge, Mass., 1952

Whyte, William Foote, *Street Corner Society the social structure of an Italian slum*, University of Chicago Press, Chicago, 1943

Wilkins, Mira, *The emergence of multinational enterprise: American business abroad from the colonial era to 1914,* Harvard University Press, Cambridge, Mass., 1970

Wilkins, Mira and Hill, Frank E., *American Business Abroad Ford on Six Continents*, Wayne State U.P., Detroit, 1964

Wilkins, Mira (ed.), *The Growth of Multinationals,* Edward Elgar Publishing Limited, Hants, England, 1991

Williams, Michael, *Ford & Fordson Tractors,* Blandford Press, Dorset and Sydney, 1985

Zweig, Ferdynand, *The British Worker,* Harmondsworth Penguin, London, 1952

Theses

Brockie, Edward G.P., 'The Rise of the Catholic Middle Classes in Ireland', MA thesis, University College Cork, 1980

D'Alton, Ian, 'Southern Irish Unionism: A Study of Cork City and County Unionists, 1885-1914', MA thesis, University College Cork, 1972

Fahy, Angela M., 'A Social Geography of Nineteenth Century Cork', MA thesis, University College Cork, 1981

Gough, Michael J., 'A History of the Physical Development of Cork City', MA thesis, University College Cork, 1973

Hartigan, Maureen, 'Irish Emigration 1931-1961: an examination of the factors which influenced emigration in this period with particular reference to the war years', MA thesis, University College Cork, 1990

Lahiff, Edward P., 'Industry and Labour in Cork, 1890-1921', MA thesis, University College Cork, 1988

Lennon, Michael John, 'Residential segregation in Cork city: 1901-1946', MA thesis, University College Cork, 2000

Linehan, Thomas A., 'The Development of Cork's Economy and Business Attitudes 1910-1939', MA thesis, University College Cork, 1985

Lucy, Dermot J., 'Cork Public Opinion and the First World War', MA thesis, University College Cork, 1972

Reddick, Stephen, 'Political and Industrial Labour in Cork 1899-1914', MA thesis, University College Cork, 1984

Stack, Eilis C., 'The physical, social and economic development of Cork city in the nineteenth century', MA thesis, University College Cork, 1996